# CALL

# AN

# AUDIBLE

DARON K. ROBERTS

# CALL

# AN

# AUDIBLE

LET MY PIVOT FROM
**HARVARD LAW** TO **NFL COACH**
INSPIRE YOUR TRANSITION

RIVER GROVE
BOOKS

Published by River Grove Books
Austin, TX
www.rivergrovebooks.com

Distributed by River Grove Books

Design and composition by Greenleaf Book Group
Cover design by Greenleaf Book Group
Images used on cover ©iStockphoto.com/OSTILL
Illustrations by Dante' "Ali Guudmon" Johnson (@aliguudmon)

Cataloging-in-Publication data is available.

Print ISBN: 978-1-63299-106-5

eBook ISBN: 978-1-63299-107-2

First Edition

*To my infinitely patient and loving wife, Hilary,*
*and to the rambunctious members of the Donut Council—*
*Dylan, Sydney, Jack, and Delaney*

**AU·DI·BLE** (NOUN)—

*a sudden change in the offensive play*
*called by the quarterback at the line of scrimmage*

*What's on the other side of fear?*

—JAMIE FOXX

# TABLE OF CONTENTS

# ACKNOWLEDGMENTS

I am grateful to Kirt and Gwen Roberts for raising me in a family that encouraged risk over comfort. I thank Kent Lance for helping me to embrace the joy of chasing the unknown. To my editor, Brandy Savarese, thank you for tolerating my early-morning and late-night rants—you helped me to crystallize my thoughts and sharpen my words. And finally, to my sister, the first woman to show me what good writing looks and smells like, I extend my gratitude.

# JUST GET IN THE BUILDING

During the summer of 2006, I was stuck on a conveyor belt that churned through Harvard Law School and made frequent deposits at corporate law firms across the country. Sandwiched between my classmates, I looked to the left and to the right for my own destination. The firms seemed indistinguishable to me—all of them shared an affinity for ampersands in their names, featured a uniformly boring clientele, and reeked of monotony. But I was a student at Harvard Law School, the most prestigious school in the universe. People at Harvard Law School clerked at law firms. That was the arrangement. So, I returned to the state of my birth—Texas—to work in the salt mines of a prestigious law firm.

On my first day at one firm, a junior associate strolled into my office and asked, "Hey, Daron, wanna grab lunch?" I was blown away. Perhaps I was on the fast track to becoming a partner? It was the first day of my clerkship and I was already getting invitations for lunch. After barely stammering a "yes," I attempted to get back to the day's work. When noon arrived, we jumped into the associate's something-series BMW and headed to the restaurant.

During an overpriced lunch at a swanky Houston steak house, I started asking questions about how the associate enjoyed his work. The answer I feared most rolled right off his tongue like an easy layup: "It's fine." The slight altar-boy pitch accompanied by an effortless shrug gave away his ambivalence for the work.

When the check arrived, he concluded our lunch by saying, "The best part about the summer is being able to eat on the firm's dime." In that moment it all became clear: Taking a summer clerk to lunch was literally a "meal ticket," and I was the write-off.

Accepting my immediate fate, I did what any overachiever would do. I gorged for the rest of the summer on breakfast tacos, Kobe beef, and swordfish. I returned to Massachusetts for my last year of law school with an extra ten pounds around my waist and a profound uncertainty about my future.[1]

At the end of my clerkship, I sat on my couch with my eyelids shut as I hit the replay button on my summer experiences. Unlike most of my fellow summer associates, I had somewhat enjoyed my work. By "enjoy," I mean that typing at my desk each day did not feel like the pain of a thousand needles shooting through my fingers. Nevertheless, I was struck by the endless reel of testimonials I had heard from young associates during overpriced and underseasoned lunches. *None* of my colleagues seemed excited about their careers, and the overwhelming majority of them were truly unhappy.

---

1    Okay, I actually gained thirteen pounds. But I justified the weight gain because I had barely survived the North American Blizzard of 2006 earlier that year. I was not going to be caught during the upcoming winter without a few more layers of fat.

It wasn't just the firm that was sending them down the drain. Each seemed to have a tangible sense of regret about choosing law over another route. At some point in their lives, the internal GPS had said "take a left" but the external GPS told them that taking the right was the more practical route. Now, overburdened with sandbags of law school debt, mortgages, and private-school tuitions for their kids, they were merely punching the clock and phoning it in. Like them— though earlier in the trajectory—I was also completely ambivalent about my chosen profession. And, in the moment of reflection as I headed into my last year of school, my disinterest scared me.

As I looked back at the pivotal moments in my life, one feeling stood out above all others: unbridled anticipation for the next step. When I graduated from the University of Texas and boarded a Greyhound bus for the cross-country ride to an internship on Capitol Hill, my stomach did flips for the entire 1,200 miles. I couldn't wait to see the Washington Monument. Similarly, when I set foot in the Texas Capitol on my first day as a legislative intern, I was giddy with excitement.

But as I reflected on my future as Daron K. Roberts, Esq., my heart rate was nearly flatlining and nothing seemed to send it spiking. That's when I received the phone call that would turn my linear life into a Jackson Pollock production. My high school football buddy, Alfonso Longoria, had a simple suggestion: "Let's take a road trip."

Alfonso and I had formed a bond as players for the Mount Pleasant Tigers. Unfortunately, we were both victims of the insurmountable size-deficit disorder that claims the college-football dreams of so many high school players. He was a short offensive guard and I was a skinny strong safety.

But in that moment, Alfonso was inviting me back to the sport I had divorced after high school graduation.

■ ■ ■

Growing up amid the piney woods of East Texas, I was practically born with a passion for Friday-night showdowns. Football games were the landmark events of my childhood. Every weekend was like a Macy's Thanksgiving Day Parade, with marching band and drum line performances. One by one, the players would enter the stadium as if conjured by some high priest of sport. First, a distant but incessant thumping would give way to a legion of band members, punching the Texas air with sharp notes and thuds of anticipation. Then the color guard arrived, flanking the band. Next came the dance team and cheerleaders and then, finally, the football team emerged from the locker room.

I spent the autumn weeks of my childhood in anticipation of watching my hometown heroes take the field on Fridays. That my athletic skills were limited is an understatement. With average speed, average quickness, and average size, I seized the only category that could make me competitive—work ethic. As a country boy, I didn't have a bevy of neighborhood kids with whom to play impromptu basketball and football games. If you stood on my roof and drew an imaginary circle with a half-mile radius, you would have a grand total of five potential pickup guys. Most of them were considerably older than me and had better things to do than play with a scrawny son of a preacher. This lack of playing experience created a mild form of insecurity in my athletic skills.

The two driving forces in my life didn't leave much room for sports, anyway. Academics and church were the uprights in the Roberts family's end zone. If I wasn't at choir practice or prayer meeting or usher meeting or any other meeting for that matter, then I was probably studying. My parents didn't just read to me; they managed the Roberts School for the Boy. Writing assignments, computer projects, and themed road trips (most notably a trek across the South to visit Civil War battlefields)—not football training camps—were my summer activities.

Another thing that had a lasting impact was that my dad never watched an entire NFL game from beginning to end. Much of his drive-by viewing can be attributed to a schedule that called for him to visit the sick and attend afternoon services. But part of it had its roots in an honorable indifference. As the son of a Baptist preacher and an elementary school principal, I lived in a household where there was little room for deviation. Both of my parents had bachelor's degrees and placed a great emphasis on education. So, while I loved football, I always knew that my boarding pass for success would be issued by academics.

. . .

Knowing that I'd never play a single down in college, I turned my sights toward achieving academic excellence.[2] Stanford University had been my first choice since my parents had taken me to Dallas for an informational session during my freshman year. Sitting near the front of a nondescript hotel ballroom, I watched the idyllic images of Palo Alto dance across a projector screen. Ten seconds into the video, I was sold. B-roll images of kids sunbathing among Span-

---

2    I did, however, receive a football scholarship offer to Austin College in Sherman, Texas. Austin College's mascot is the kangaroo. I declined the offer.

ish-tiled cathedrals of higher education enchanted me. On the trip back to Mount Pleasant, I swore an oath to submit an early-decision application to Stanford. If I got in, I was obligated to accept.

Two years later, an oversize envelope from Palo Alto arrived. I got in. My fastest unofficial forty-yard-dash time was clocked on November 12, 1996, as I bolted up the driveway from my mailbox to the front door. The only complication was the price tag.

This shifted my focus back to Texas. As a fifth-generation Texan, I loved my state, but I was ready to leave. The University of Texas was the second option on my list, but a scholarship interview one weekend shifted my mindset. With big dreams of becoming the governor of my home state, I accepted a full academic scholarship to UT. The Forty Acres, a moniker for the University of Texas main campus, felt surprisingly like home. I jumped into the throes of a liberal arts education and closed the door (or so I thought) on my romance with football.

## A GROWN MAN GOES TO SUMMER CAMP

It had been nearly ten years since I made my final play on the Mount Pleasant football team, so when Alfonso—now a high school football coach—called to invite me to join him at the Steve Spurrier Football Camp in South Carolina, I was immediately reminded of the smell of a freshly cut field, echoes of the drumroll before kickoff, and the uncontrollable thumping of my heart during a halftime speech. I leapt at the chance to reenter the world that I had so loved as a child.

By day, I was tasked with coaching fifth-grade players. By night, I was a chaperone, making sure the kids didn't break curfew. One night, as I sat with the young men in the commons area of that old dormitory talking about girlfriends, video games, and why a lawyer-to-be was coaching fifth graders at a football camp, I listened as a white kid from the right side of the tracks talked with a black kid from the wrong side of the tracks. As inquisition grew into discussion, the two boys realized they had more in common than they thought. It was as if Holden Caulfield and the Invisible Man met each other for the first time only to discover that they were actually long-lost twins separated at birth. The melanin divide evaporated as the boys discovered they were really the same person. In that moment, I felt my career dreams almost instantly morph into the desire to become a football coach. Three days working a football camp was just the reality check that I needed. My ~~passion~~ purpose had smacked me in the face. It fell in my lap wrapped in a thirteen-pound pigskinned oval.

■ ■ ■

Back in Cambridge, a large majority of my classmates laughed at me.[3] Back in Texas, my family members wondered if I needed to see a psychiatrist. But I kept drafting my exit strategy. Sitting at the same desk at which I had penned legal briefs, I wrote letters to football programs across the country, ~~asking~~ begging for an internship. Legalese would not work. None of my recipients wanted to hear about the arc of First Amendment case law. This letter needed to convey my desire without coming off as starry-eyed and naive. It also needed to demonstrate my willingness to go broke on sweat equity.

Still, I struggled. The blinking cursor just stared at me. Why was this so hard? I realized I had not written about myself since completing

---

3    With the notable exceptions of Professor David Wilkins, Shaun Jacob Mathew, Taj Wilson, John Mathews II, Cole Wiley, Amanda Edwards, Alex Lee, Antonia Floyd, and Diane Lucas.

law school applications years earlier. Every assignment I had in law school hinged on intellectual detachment. I had spent the last three years as an observer. Now it was time to be intentional and personal.

The cursor morphed into a flashing smirk. I had to fight back. I began to type.

*Dear Coach,*

*I am a third-year student at Harvard Law School and I want to become a football coach. After three days of working as a volunteer coach at the Steve Spurrier Football Camp, I realized that changing the life trajectories of young men can be fulfilled by coaching a sport that I fell in love with in high school. I understand that you receive countless letters each year but I promise I will work harder than anyone else you are considering for this position.*

*For the past two years, I have immersed myself in the study of the law in the world's most challenging institution of higher learning. This quest required that I spend sleepless nights in the library toiling through legal cases.*

*Notwithstanding the heavy workload, I devoted every fiber of my spirit to this academic pursuit. Now, I want to take this same work ethic to your organization. I am committed to performing any menial task at any arbitrary hour in order to add value to the team. Please consider me for any entry-level position that you may have available.*

*Sincerely,*

*Daron K. Roberts*

I reviewed what I had written. What the hell was I doing? My classmates were headed to law firms on Wall Street and clerkships with federal judges. I was hoping to go wherever a head coach was nutty enough to let me in the building.

With the click of a Print button, I began a direct mail campaign to get into the NFL, sending letters to every NFL team. I searched through the online directory of coaches at every NFL team and tried to find a personal connection. Was the coach born in Texas? Did he study government in college? Any common ground that I could find was fair game. I just needed one hook. To think that ten years earlier, I had figured my first direct mail campaign would be to fund a race for state representative.

My football goal of a training camp internship was much, much lower than election to public office, but nearly as difficult to attain. A training camp intern is essentially plankton, functioning at the bottom of the food chain. The list of your potential responsibilities includes ferrying players to and from the airport, setting out cones before practice, holding tackling dummies during practice, and picking up cones after practice. It is not a position of glory and acclaim, but it was exactly what I wanted.

Securing an internship was even more daunting given the fact that I had not played football in college—let alone in the NFL—*and* that I had spent the previous three years in law school. Almost as soon as I placed a letter in the mailbox, I'd receive a rejection letter. It was a rough period, but I got through it by repeating one statement upon waking up each day: "Just get in the building."

Gaining no traction as a training camp intern, I started searching for real openings in ticket sales departments and community relations departments. If I could just get in the building, I would outwork my peers (remember, I was one of those "try-hard" guys on the football team) and gain a foothold in the organization. I hung signs in my apartment: "Get in the Building." I would repeat the words to myself in the mirror thirty-two times after brushing my teeth, "Get in the building. Get in the building," and so on. I changed the background picture on my laptop to read, "Get in the Building."

My roommate, Ernesto Martinez, was a good sport (pun intended). He casually suggested, "Maybe we should tape the rejection letters up in your room? That way, you can get used to it and it won't feel so bad?" Perhaps Ernesto was right; as rejection letters continued to fill my mailbox, I drew on a formative experience from my undergrad days.[4] When I ran for student government president at UT, people told me I had no chance of being elected. Their justification? I was from Mount Pleasant, an unknown town with a population of only 12,291. (The enrollment at UT at that time was not only the largest in the country, but it was four times the population of my hometown.) Traditionally, student body presidents shared three features. They hailed from Texas metroplexes (Houston or Dallas), they were male, and they were white. I was one for three. As a reminder of my low odds of winning, I wrote a simple message on my bathroom mirror: "No one thinks you're going to win but you."

I won.

During my senior year at UT, I applied to Harvard Law School. I applied to other schools as well, heeding the advice of admissions gurus to create buckets: Wish List, Safety Schools, and Sure Things. But in reality, I was only willing to go to Harvard. My first application was placed on "hold"—a purgatory where listless souls wander until

---

4    To receive a customized rejection letter, visit www.rejectmenow.com.

their number is called. I never got the call. When I applied the second time, I made the wait list. On a whim, I decided to make a "cold visit" to the law school. It was 2002 and I was working on Capitol Hill for Senator Joe Lieberman.

I called in sick and jumped on a plane from Washington to Boston. I sat in the lobby of the admissions office, waiting to speak with someone—anyone. I finally got three minutes with a woman who was kind in a very hurry-up-and-leave-so-I-can-keep-reading-applications sort of way. She assured me there was nothing more I could do to alter my chances of getting elevated from the wait list. I thanked her and headed back to Logan airport.

And the third year? Wait-listed again. At this point, everyone but my parents told me to just go to another law school. Columbia, Georgetown, NYU, and UT were all excellent options. People—none of whom had signed up to underwrite my tuition—asked, "Are you too good for other schools?" A recurrent argument made by my "supporters" was that if I kept waiting, I'd be thirty by the time I graduated from law school. In response, I would ask, "How old will I be in five years if I don't go to Harvard Law School?" I couldn't change my birthdate but I could marshal every ounce of my effort to keep knocking, and I did.

I wanted to go to Harvard Law School and I was willing to wait. After *three* rounds of being wait-listed, I was finally accepted.

So during my letter-writing campaign of 2006, I drew resolve from my record of "beating the house" when the cards were stacked against me. Nearing graduation, I finally received the call that I had been waiting for.

"Daron, this is Herm Edwards."

Pause.

Pause.

More pause. I couldn't make my voice work.

"Daron?" asked Coach Edwards.

"Yes, Coach Edwards, I'm here," I stuttered.

"I don't know why you want to do this," he said. "Lord knows why a soon-to-be Harvard Law grad wants to coach football, but I've got a training camp internship for you if you want it."

"Absolutely, I want it," I said without hesitation.

"Good, I'll have my guy call you to set up the details." And with that, he hung up.

After the call ended, I sat on the edge of my bed and thought about what had just happened. Herm Edwards, head coach of the Kansas City Chiefs, had just called *me*!

To say that the "compensation" paled in comparison to the $150,000 offers of employment would be an understatement. The equation looked something like this:

$$0 < \$150,000$$

Coach Edwards's guy gave me the rundown. No benefits. Eighteen-hour workdays would be my life, but if I wanted to make it, this was my "in." Although I had already placed a hefty deposit down for bar examination preparatory courses, I was in.

I was *all in*. Why? In the fall of 2006, I was dumb enough to not care about the statistical challenge before me.

## PIVOT POINTS

Do you dream about making a dramatic change in your life or career? It is incredibly difficult for driven, highly educated young professionals who have long-held visions for where they *should* be in their professional and personal lives to call an audible.

I hope my story illustrates that if you find yourself ready to change course, you just have to put your foot on the very lowest rung of whatever ladder you want to climb and prepare yourself for a relentless ascent. In the chapters that follow, I will highlight the pivot points that I learned in my own climb to help you make the journey to the top rung. By no means am I so delusional as to think this process will be easy for you. Life is complicated. Mortgages, college loans, and kids are just a few of the realities that can complicate a clear path from point A to point B. But I hope my story can provide a few pivot points to help you begin that journey.

# CHAPTER 1

# REMEMBER:
# FIRST IN. LAST OUT.

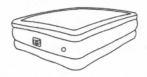

As I prepared for my journey from Mount Pleasant, Texas, to Kansas City, Missouri, for training camp, I was transported back seven months to standing on the deck of the *Lyubov Orlova* as she disembarked from Tierra del Fuego, en route to Antarctica.[5] Named after the godmother of Russian cinema, the thirty-year-old ship wore her age well. We lurched southward into the outer stretches of Chilean

---

5    At the time of publication, the *Lyubov Orlova* was lost at sea. According to *Telegraph* reporter Gregg Morgan, "The deserted Mariya Yermolova–class cruise ship was being transported from Canada to the Dominican Republic to be scrapped in January of [2013] when a tow cable broke, leaving her adrift in the Atlantic Ocean." http://www.telegraph.co.uk/news /newsvideo/weirdnewsvideo/10591757/Rat-infested-ghost-ship-Lyubov-Orlova-heading-for-Britain.html

waters, headed to Antarctica, the sixth continent on my bucket list of visiting all seven before turning thirty. School was in session, but I had strategically chosen classes that called for a research paper in lieu of a final exam. So, instead of sitting in a sterile classroom listening to a professor drone on about bankruptcy law, I decided it was time for me to cross off bucket list item number six. I was twenty-eight—the thirtieth year of my existence on earth was approaching more quickly than I wanted to accept.

Standing on that Russian ship and heading for islands of ice, my heart was beating to the tempo of a Motown groove. I was giddy. The hairs on my neck stood at attention. I was short of breath. These symptoms were less a result of the crisp air and more a byproduct of anticipation. That feeling—the irrepressible sucker punch of plunging into the unknown without a British-accented GPS voice calling the shots or a sanitized "Let's Go" guidebook planning my itinerary—was palpable. I could taste it. It reminded me of my first swig of whiskey. The initial bite, the cascade of tingles, and the eventual warming of the chest were real to me. On the contrary, sitting in a civil procedure class was a bitter pill. There was no warming of the chest.

My impending departure for NFL training camp brought back all of those gut-tightening and sweetly anxious feelings. After kissing my mother goodbye and hugging my dad, I pointed my road-worn Tahoe to the northeast up Highway 271 into Oklahoma. The butterflies had returned. I was excited for the next step.

# A GROWN MAN RETURNS TO SUMMER CAMP

I zipped through the Sooner State, at times clocking over eighty miles per hour down the Indian Nation Turnpike, eating up the miles to Kansas City. Crossing the Missouri state line provided the prick to my psyche that I needed for the final push.

Lamonte Winston, executive director of player development for the Kansas City Chiefs, met me upon my arrival. He is one of the founding fathers of NFL player development. Player development involves cultivating and honing players' skills to ensure success long after the last touchdown. His passion for the game was evident in his words, but what was even more tangible was his desire to guide men from helmets to healthy lifestyles. Lamonte was concerned with ensuring that players would transition into a rewarding life once their football value had been reduced to zero. In a league where the average tenure was 3.5 years, many players had spent at least twenty years preparing for a profession that would last for only three. The shock of returning to society without a ball in hand—similar to the post-traumatic stress disorder experienced by our service members after returning from battle—could be debilitating. Lamonte was standing at the front door when a rookie landed on the doorsteps of Arrowhead Stadium and he would be the last to shake a player's hand when a player was traded or cut.

Lamonte offered his hand. "So, you're the Hahvud guy?" he asked.

"I guess you could say that," I said, shrugging. I should have known that, like it or not, I'd become known by my alma mater.

Lamonte welcomed me to the Land of the Chiefs and promptly checked me into the team hotel. The only perk of staying at the hotel, notwithstanding the free rent, was its proximity to Arrowhead Stadium. We would stay in Kansas City for a week and then head to River Falls, Wisconsin, for training camp. Upon entering my room, I met Grady Brown, who would be my roommate for the next two weeks. In the regular season, Grady was a defensive backs coach at Alabama A&M University, and he still looked as if he could throw on a pair of shoulder pads and play.

"So, where you coming from?" Grady asked.

"Mount Pleasant, Texas. Well, that's my hometown, but I've spent the past five years in Boston," I replied.

"Oh, who were you coaching with? BU or BC?"

"Well, neither," I explained. "I was in grad school and then law school."

"Law school?" he asked. "Where?"

"Harvard."

"Harvard? What in the hell are you doing here? You trying to be a GM?"

"Nope, I want to be a coach. I want to coach defensive backs."

"Man, that's nuts! I definitely was not ready for that." Grady laughed. "Well, you teach me a little law, and I will teach you a little ball, deal?"

"No doubt, let's do it."

We instantly became friends.

Over the course of the next few days, I had that same exchange many times. My first encounters at Arrowhead consisted of quizzical looks from the staff—everyone from equipment managers to the defensive coordinator. I was the "Hahvud guy" and people took great pleasure in practicing their Southie accents on me.

But my badge of honor quickly became a scarlet letter. It would be an understatement to say that skepticism was the general consensus among my compatriots. I realized that I would have to combat the perception that I was a disgruntled attorney who was looking for a coaching job as an escape from the corporate world. My approach was simple: I would diplomatically stalk the coaches and demonstrate through my actions that I was serious about my future in the League. This was not a summer escapade. I was playing the long game.

The one activity that consumed the majority of a coach's time was watching film. During training camp, a coach was looking at the tape of opponents the team would play in the fall. During the season, a coach was looking at the film from the most recent game as well as film of the upcoming opponent. During the offseason, the coach was looking at the college tapes of players entering the NFL Draft. The process never ended. As I walked the halls I could easily recognize when a coach was looking at tape. The room would seem dark at first glance from the hallway but, on closer inspection, I could see the faint glow of the projector. I would just walk into the office and sit down in the back. If two or more coaches were together, I would never intrude, just in case they were discussing trade secrets. But if the coach was solo, I was going to quietly take advantage of the learning opportunity.

My tape-stalking mission was a two-pronged approach. First, it would show the coaches that I was interested in their work. Second, I would learn how to analyze film—arguably the primary activity of football coaches.

I learned a lot from observing the film-watching technique of one particular coach—Tim Krumrie, our defensive line coach. From my research on "Krummie," I learned he was considered to be a true tough guy. He played for twelve seasons as a defensive lineman for the Cincinnati Bengals. When the Bengals played the San Francisco 49ers in Super Bowl XXIII, Krumrie broke his leg so severely that the medics had to use an inflatable splint to stabilize it on the field. Most players—even tough players—would have acquiesced to leaving the field for a trip to the emergency room after snapping their leg in two. But he refused to leave the stadium, and he sat in agony watching the game from the Bengals locker room. The Bengals eventually lost, but his story became the type of legend the NFL is built on.

Given Krummie's history as a player and reputation for being a defensive line tactician, I knew I could learn a lot from him. He would zoom in on the moment that a defensive end turned the edge on his way to sacking the quarterback. Over and over, he would press the rewind button. As he watched and rewatched, he would grunt in various tones that would communicate his evaluation of the technique on display. A flat grunt meant the player had taken an easy approach and was missing an opportunity to outmaneuver the less athletic offensive lineman who stood between him and a sack. A high-pitched grunt meant there was something Krumrie liked—that he had noticed some nearly imperceptible aspect of physics combined with geometry and mixed with a tinge of relentlessness that piqued his interest. As I learned to match the subtleties of his vocalizations with what I saw on the film, I began to develop my own philosophy of what worked for a defensive lineman. I spent that week leading up to our departure on a "soak in" mission, to blend into the artwork and digest all of the information that I could wrap my eyes and ears around. I filled two notebooks in seven days with observations and first impressions.

During the week leading up to our departure for training camp, I made it my mission to learn everyone's names. Armed with flash cards that I had made by printing profile pictures from the team's website, I would camp out in the hotel bathroom and work through the names and faces of everyone from the assistant general manager to the communications director. Why the bathroom? Because it offered refuge from Grady's curious gaze. Fearful of being viewed as a complete putz, I commandeered the toilet seat as my study hall. By the first day of training camp, I had memorized thirty-eight names.

In addition to learning everyone's names, I made a list of five personal goals to ensure that my debut did not end up as a finale.

1   Find three champions.
2   Keep a notepad in my pocket **at all times**.
3   Carry two pens, two pencils, and two Sharpies (one red and one black) **at all times**.
4   Get to the gym every morning by 4:45 a.m.
5   Talk to Herm at least once a day.

In the moment, I thought my five goals were things that a would-be coach had to do in order to stay in the building. Looking back, however, I see that my goals could fit into the pursuit of any dream job. If you're trying to break into a new career, your main objective must be to "stick." You want the sum of your personality and work ethic to make it difficult for an organization to let you go.

# FIND THREE CHAMPIONS

I have always bristled at the notion of having a "circle" of friends. A circle feels too big to manage. I prefer to convert the circle into a triangle. With three key people in my corner, I would have enough support to guide me through the labyrinth of the Chiefs organization and help me to secure the full-time gig that would keep me in the NFL.

Finding influencers in an organization can be a challenging task. And it's important to remember that an influencer is not someone who simply offers encouragement—it is someone who can make things happen. Very seldom does an accurate map of the influencers in an organization overlap with the organizational chart, so it's critical to listen to and watch who is making decisions to uncover who has real leverage in an organization.

# THE NOTEPAD

Leading up to my departure for Kansas City, I initiated a reconnaissance mission. I read every book on coaching that I could find. I consumed Jon Gruden's *Do You Love Football?!*, Bill Walsh's *The Score Takes Care of Itself*, and Neil Hayes's *When the Game Stands Tall*, all within a week. From there, I moved on to John Wooden's *Wooden on Leadership*, Bob Lamonte's *Winning the NFL Way*, and David Maraniss's *When Pride Still Mattered* the next week. I wanted to accumulate as much insider information as I could before starting my internship. The one takeaway that kept surfacing from my reading was the need to have a constant form of taking notes. With the potential embarrassment of a cell phone ringing during a meeting too likely, I embraced the pocket-size spiral notepad.

# TWO PENS, TWO PENCILS, TWO SHARPIES

Unlike the notebook, the pens weren't for me—they were for the coaches around me. I was certain that someone was going to need a pen, and I was going to be the person to offer one.

I seldom used a pen. I wanted the ability to erase because I knew my error quotient would be relatively high in my coaching start-up phase. The pencil was my best friend. I wrote down everything I saw, heard, and felt. Did a prepractice speech go over well? Was Troy picking up the defense quickly enough? How many cones did Krummie need for defensive line drills? I wrote at angles. I used shorthand. I wrote in verse. I circled, starred, and underlined like a man with a publisher's deadline. Each night, I would transcribe my scribblings into well-defined notes organized into buckets (Defensive Strategy, Scheduling, Crisis Management, Injury Protocol, Handling the Media, and Leadership). I was building a library of notes that I could reference as I built my coaching career.

In the coaching universe, the Sharpie is an essential tool of the trade. In the late nights before a practice, coaches would spend long hours drawing "practice cards," diagrams of offensive and defensive plays that would be executed during the following day's practice. Passing routes, running lanes, and blocking assignments would collide on an 8.5 × 11 sheet of card stock. Invariably, during a practice session, a coach would have to make an adjustment to his cards. I wanted to be the go-to guy for anyone needing a Sharpie.

My pen preparation made me the Steve Urkel of the coaching world. I wore one pencil clipped to my collar.[6] Two Sharpies were

6    For background information on Steve Urkel, visit Wikipedia.

clipped on the left pocket of my shorts, and on the right pocket were two Pilot Precise V5 pens and the remaining pencil. I was armed for battle. Our equipment manager would always tease, "Are you some starving artist?" I shrugged it off, though. I knew he'd ask me for a pen before the camp was over.

## THE GYM

I have always had difficulty sleeping, seldom getting more than five hours of rest a night. After spending fifteen years trying every sleeping pill and every concoction that I could find online, I decided to just give in and make my early mornings productive. Thus, each morning, I crept out of my dorm room in Grimm Hall and made the trek across the River Falls campus to work out at 4:45 a.m. Based on my research on Herm, I knew that he also adhered to a strict work-out regimen and that I would likely find him at the gym. Remember, Herm was a critical point on my triangle of support. Running into Herm at the gym killed three birds with one stone: talking to Herm, working out, and cultivating a major point in my triangle of influencers.

## THE GRIND

Camp was grueling and chaotic, but I was determined to rise to the challenge. One coach, Mike Priefer, immediately noticed me hanging around during practice. He couldn't avoid it—I was always asking if there was anything that I could do to help. After a couple of days of "no," he finally relented and rattled off a few directives on where to place a series of orange cones. I scribbled the notes in my notebook and ran off to fulfill my orders.

Prief was not pleased. He promptly started moving cones and coaching me on my errors. I scribbled more notes. By day six, I had become a professional cone layer. Building on that success, I began to pick up additional tasks like catching the practice snaps of our long snapper, Jean-Philippe Darche, who would rifle snaps from fifteen yards. It took a few days for me to get accustomed to the force of the snapper's darts, but I finally got the hang of it.

As a roving jack-of-all-tasks eager to become indispensable, I pestered as many people as I possibly could. For example, if I saw the offensive line coach putting practice bags out, I'd ask if he needed a hand. The first plea would always elicit the same response: "No." But after a few days, I'd get the telltale shrug from a coach—indicating that my persistence had paid off—and then I'd be put to work holding bags, retrieving footballs, acting as a tackling dummy. You name it, I did it. I wasn't so much a human as I was another piece of practice equipment. And in reality, that's exactly what I wanted. I needed to blend in and become an indispensable part of the operation.

■ ■ ■

Herm made it clear to me that after the second preseason game, my internship would be officially over. Because the sheer demand for coaching positions could not keep up with the relatively low turn-over, Herm wanted to manage my expectations. Always looking for clues in the team paperwork (I was also the copier jockey), I saw a flight reservation that had my name on it. But I couldn't accept my dismissal. I had absolutely nothing to return to. Of course, my parents would have allowed me to play the "recent-grad-trying-to-figure-it-out" card for a few months and to camp out in my childhood bedroom, but I had too much pride to play that hand.

I had one toe inside the building and I had no intention of leaving. Camp was coming to an end and there were three days left until we were slated to return to Kansas City. I decided that I had only one chance at getting retained for the season. I needed to go to the top— every day—and convince Herm that he needed me.

I cobbled together every argument I could think of and drafted my plea. It was time to put that six-figure, Harvard Law education to the test. Here was my approach:

Day 1: "Coach, you know that Coach Priefer doesn't have anyone to help him with special teams."

Day 2: "You wouldn't need to buy any equipment for me. I'll use my personal laptop to get stuff done."

Day 3: "I don't have to eat with the team, I'll bring my lunch every day."

To put it simply, I would volunteer for the team. I didn't need an office (or even a salary). I just wanted the chance to work. I'd keep my mouth shut and do any task—no matter how small. I'd be the first person in the door and the last one out. My sole mission was to make life easier for the coaching staff and equip them with more time to work with the people who mattered most: the players.

As I stood on the practice field and prepared to offer up my final pitch to Herm, my legs were shaking. Fortunately, it was a windy day, so I am not sure that Herm could tell that I was nervous. I controlled the tenor of my voice by mentally tightening the "quiver" valve that was desperately trying to burst out.

My courage was engaged in hand-to-hand combat with the usual suspects: self-doubt and fear. Saying each word required all the mental strength I could muster. I thought of my nameless compatriots—interns at the other thirty-one clubs—who I'm sure had spent countless nights rehearsing very similar speeches in front of their mirrors. Something kept them from getting to this stage. Maybe the naysayers had extinguished the necessary hope to make a case. But here I was, ready to make the most important pitch of my life.

It was no surprise that Herm was reluctant to let me stay, and it was easy to understand his reasoning. He didn't want to set a precedent that would open the Arrowhead doors to every intern that came through. But I was determined to be the exception. I had spent every morning of camp in front of the bathroom mirror repeating to myself: "You're staying in the NFL. You're staying in the NFL. You're staying in the NFL."

After much consternation, Herm struck a deal with me. The terms: I would volunteer with the Chiefs for the 2007 season on the contingency that I also dedicated my time to the Bishop Miege High School football team. Coach Edwards called up his good friend Tim Grunhard, a former NFL center and the head coach of the Stags, to get me set up. The private school was a twenty-three-minute commute across the Missouri/Kansas border. I would work with the Chiefs from 5 a.m. until 3 p.m., drive to Bishop Miege, coach there until 6 p.m., and then head back to Arrowhead to finish up my work. Here was the compensation package: No pay. No benefits. Eighteen-hour days.

I had only one question: "Where do I sign?"

Thinking back on that day, I often imagine how Herm would have responded had I bristled at the idea of splitting time between the Chiefs and a high school gig on the other side of town. When I told one of my friends about the terms of Herm's "offer," he asked, "Why would you do that? Don't you just want to be in the NFL?" Sure, I could have told Herm that I was only interested in coaching in the League. I have countless friends who have turned down potentially life-changing opportunities because they thought they were "above the work."

One instance in particular stands out for me. A friend really wanted to open a brewery. He consumed as many books and videos on the topic as he could find and decided that taking a part-time job in a brewery would be the best way to break in. There were just a few issues: He had two kids and a full-time job as an attorney. Undeterred, he convinced the owner of a local brewery to give him a shot. His first assignment included mopping the floors. This proved to be too "menial" for him and he promptly returned to the firm, where, you might say, he does more white-collar housekeeping.

We all have friends who really want to break into a profession but are above the "mailroom" entry point. They would rather hang on to their plush corner office and languish in boredom and despair than parachute to the bowels of a profession and work their way up. Not me. I recognized my opportunity as a way to gain valuable experience as a coach. I would gladly trade twenty years of drudgery for two years of long days and low pay.

Up until that point, the Chiefs had put up all of the training camp interns in a hotel. It wasn't a four-star accommodation but it was close, convenient, and, most importantly, free. Now that I was on the full-time staff, I was on my own to find lodging. In a moment of inspiration, I decided that the best course of action was to live at Arrowhead during the week. I went on Craigslist.org, found a cheap basement rental for $250, and signed a month-to-month lease. But I didn't have any intention of living there. I just needed a home base to store some of my things. I bought an inflatable Coleman twin mattress, a set of sheets, and a pillow and returned to the stadium to locate an inconspicuous spot to sleep each night. I even timed the logistics of inflating and deflating the mattress: just under four minutes. It could be folded and placed behind the desk quickly and easily whenever necessary. I descended into the basement of Arrowhead to find my new apartment. I needed to be the first person in the office every single day.

I immediately scratched a few rooms off my list. The quarterbacks, offensive linemen, defensive backs, and linebackers tended to study tape after hours. The last thing I wanted was to get a surprise wake-up call from the starting quarterback. This left the rooms of the running backs, wide receivers, and defensive linemen to investigate. The running backs were the team practical jokers. Scratch. Wide receivers? They were equally unpredictable. Scratch. I was left with the perfect spot—the defensive linemen's meeting room.

As I gazed up at the grimy ceiling from the comfort of my air mattress, I thought: "Here we go, Daron, let's do this."

## PIVOT POINTS

1  Find three champions—reduce your circle to a triangle.

2  Identify the influencers. Watch, listen, and take note of who moves the decision-making needle.

3  Always carry a writing instrument (or two) and notebook. Always. And no, a cell phone, laptop, or tablet will not suffice.

4  Beat your target to the "point." Determine the schedule of your main target, and make sure you beat him or her to the point every day.

5  Be willing to mop the floors. Get used to the struggle and the pain early and begin to build your immunity. Remember: No struggle, no progress.

# CHAPTER 2

# EMBRACE THE MUNDANE

## MAPPING THE ORGANIZATION:
## WHY, HOW, AND WHAT

Without the luxury of a job title or a "real" office, I was in a tricky spot. Unlike other "employees," I didn't have a one-page job description to reference when I didn't know how to occupy my time. I had to write my own job description.

Sure, I got to avoid the gauntlet of human resources meetings and paperwork that accompanies new hires, but only because I had not really been hired. I didn't have to sign a single sheet of paper to begin my work with the Chiefs. I had to figure out on my own what I needed to do and, more importantly, I had to figure out whom to target for work assignments.

I began by sketching an organizational map. An org map is like the familiar organizational chart, but on Ritalin. Beneath the names of the major players are lists of why, how, and what. The "why" is the reason that person was right for the position. The "how" is a short description of how the person got the job. And the "what" is an educated guess as to the person's end goal. So, for a coach, I may write that his "why" is that he's a former player and coaching made sense for him. The "how" is that he was brought to the team by the head coach. The "what" is that he wanted to eventually become a head coach.

My org map quickly took on the look of early drawings of the New World. As I added new staff, I would tape another 11 × 14 sheet of paper onto the original. Because I didn't have a real office, I kept my map nestled amid a pile of coaching notes. The system may have been organic—read: cobbled together—but it worked. This was a real-time exercise, and as I gathered more information, I edited my earlier impressions with new ones. It gave me a good visual of the office politics within the organization. In many ways, it forced me to think beyond the cubicles and reserved parking spots and to really unravel the reasons why the people above me (essentially every human in the building) acted the way that they did.

The map provided me with a visual base camp. I would return to it as I observed the decisions that people made on a daily basis. I believed that it was as important for me to learn the nuances of our all-out blitz package as it was to understand why a veteran player would not treat a rookie coach with respect. My scientifically untested working theory was that my ascension in the National Football League would adhere to a 70/30 split: Seventy percent of the rise could be attributed to what I knew about who I knew, and thirty percent of the rise would relate to what I knew about what I knew.

In college, I had placed an emphasis on intellect. I call this the *Atlantic Monthly* period of my life. GPAs, LSAT scores, and percentile tags mattered in that world. Now, I was in the *People* magazine period of my life. Content was important, but it was more critical to understand the motivations of those in positions I wanted for myself. I needed to know what made the people around me tick. For example, was the position coach looking to become a defensive coordinator one day? Did the former-head-coach-turned-coordinator take his current job to bide time until he could land the next head coaching job? The answers to these questions were important to help catapult me out of the basement of the organization.

## WORKING BACKWARD

On my first "official" day with the Chiefs, I sat in my "office" (really just a desk in the press box overlooking Arrowhead Stadium). I had the best view in the building. Almost 50,000 square feet of one of the most historic fields in NFL history stretched below me. It was breathtaking. And it was lonely. During the week, no one had any reason to be in the press box. Sure, on Sundays in the fall, the long rectangular room teemed with reporters, but on a Monday morning at 5 a.m., I was its sole occupant.

As I stared blankly at the sheet of paper on my desk, I decided to list the duties that I wanted to take on during my season of volunteering. Assuming the worst-case scenario (owner Clark Hunt walking into the building after our last game and firing everybody), I considered what another head coach, say, Bill Belichick, would find valuable from my "football résumé." Belichick (or, more than likely, his administrative assistant) had rejected my petitions to serve as a training camp intern, so my goal was to accumulate a bundle of experiences that would convince him—and any other skeptical head coach—to give me a job.

Here are the skill buckets I came up with:

1   Practice Gofer: Master of the practice setup and breakdown
2   King of the Copier: Make it as easy as possible for the coaching staff to get the paper they depended on
3   Film Breakdown: Analyze tape and identify key variables that coaches need to organize opponent tendencies
4   Game-Day Lieutenant: Communicate with coaches during game day

There was a logical and deliberate progression from Practice Gofer to Game-Day Lieutenant. Success on the practice field would lead to the "opportunity" to push paper in the office. Teams guarded their scouting reports and game plans with the devotion of concealing state secrets. Being entrusted with making copies was a display of trust. From that level, I would rise to watch and analyze film. And after gaining credibility as someone who could break down film, I would then move on to working games, the weekly contests that ultimately determined the fate of every coach and player in the organization.

While these skill buckets are specific to the sports industry, there are clear parallels to other worlds. Serving as a practice gofer is less a tactical skill and more of a triumph of humility. During the first two years of my time in the NFL, I had the job of setting out cones for drills before practice started. After one practice, my buddy from law school who had come to watch asked me why I had "cone duty." Because I was a grunt and part of a grunt's job was to do grunt-like duties, I told him. It was that easy for me. I was in a world where legal acumen and the ability to ace logic puzzles had very little value. The willingness to do the menial would translate into the opportunity to do the monumental. The ability to break film down is an analytical skill. Watching an opponent's game, identifying the strengths and weaknesses of both the system and the individual players, is strikingly similar to writing a legal brief. A lawyer takes the facts, filters them through precedents, and constructs the best arguments in her client's favor. Having the patience to comb through the details and minutiae in order to get a solid understanding of what to emphasize in a court brief is much the same as analyzing film to plan the next day's practice.

# KING OF THE COPIER

While most of my tasks may seem trivial to the casual observer, they were serious responsibilities in the coaching world. Without any professional or college playing or coaching experience, I needed to engender considerable trust in order to earn an opportunity to even be considered for a coaching role. To get that trust, I needed to execute every task I received with the utmost care and precision. I needed to become known as the go-to guy for anything. Players might not ask me for advice on how to improve their technique, and other coaches were not going to ask for my opinion on a play, but with each task I performed perfectly I was gradually building my reputation and credibility.

And that's how I found the copier.

There were few places in the building that coaches hated more than the copy room. For a multimillion-dollar organization, the Chiefs did not boast the world's most reliable or frankly even functional copier. The machine was constantly beeping and shutting down—both occurrences elicited the same response from an impatient coach: "What the fuck is wrong with this machine?"

After hearing this invective for the fourth time, I saw my opportunity. I knew that every coach—from the quarterbacks coach to the special teams coordinator—would have at least one copy job in the course of a day. I also knew that the ratio of coaches to grunts was high. The system needed a copier whisperer and I was just the guy.

The guys just ahead of me on the food chain were well compensated and hated dealing with the copier. To make copies was the absolute drudgery of their week. This was uncharted ground—the no-man's-land of any office building. There were no barbarians at the gate trying to nudge me off of this perch. I had found a game that I could win.

So I looked behind the copier and found the user's manual. The book was coated with a thick layer of dust. It was obvious that no one had looked at the manual since the day of installation. As I flipped through the pages, I couldn't help but chuckle. A year before, I had been reading Scalia dissents. Now, I was trying to parse error codes and clear paper jams in order to find the quickest way to make a double-sided printout.

I'm a guy with three degrees, but I spent the majority of my time in the copy room. Why? Because the copy room was the information hub of our office. Football coaches have an unhealthy attachment to paper. Of the major sports, football represents the prehistory of technological innovation. Although we had access to email and laptops and a host of other electronic devices, the coaches who sat above me on the org chart wanted everything printed. Practice schedules, meeting agendas, play diagrams, scouting reports—nothing was too big or too small for an 8.5 × 11 piece of pulp.

And so, over the course of just a few weeks, I became the go-to person for any issue related to the copy machines. Paper jam? I was the man. Can't figure out how to double-side? I was the man. Color cartridge is empty? I was the man. My "peers" called me a suck-up and made a lot of funny jokes about me. But the more they laughed, the more time I spent in the copy room. What they didn't know was that I was running a covert operation with each copy job. As the gatekeeper of copies, I got a sneak peek at the upcoming schedules, practice plans, and player lineups. And I stored all of this information away in three critical repositories: my head, my journal, and my org map.

More importantly, I was building goodwill with each job. During one of my visits to the copy room, I ran into our special teams coordinator, Coach Priefer, applying his foot to the machine. Lights were flashing, alarm bells were dinging, paper was shooting from the machine. This did not look good. With a player meeting on the horizon, Priefer needed to make additional copies for nearly every team member. I saw my opportunity.

"Coach Priefer, I can make these copies and bring them to you," I said.

"This machine is awful. Good luck. I need sixty copies of this, double-sided. Bring it to the meeting room when you're done."

That was it. He walked out.

As soon as he left the room, I whipped out my notepad and wrote down everything he had just said. Although I was confident that I wasn't going to forget the details of the simple assignment, I wasn't willing to wager my hiring prospects on the chance that I would forget. This was a big break in my world.

First, I unloaded and reloaded every paper tray in the machine. Nothing changed. Flashing lights.

I emptied the hole-punch tray.

Nothing.

As my troubleshooting list got shorter, I decided to take the plunge.

I unplugged the machine.

The cacophony quieted.

I plugged the machine back in and waited for the lights to signal signs of life, murmuring a prayer to the office gods.

My thirty seconds of prayer, which felt like thirty hours, ended in glorious silence. There were no more beeps and no more flashing lights. I placed the document on the glass and hit Start. We were in business.

With only a few seconds to spare, I raced down the stairs with ninety copies in hand. Early in my reign as king of the copier I had decided to increase any copy request by fifty percent. The equation looked something like this:

$$X + X/2 = Y$$
$$X = \text{original request}$$
$$Y = \text{final output}$$

My justification for selfishly killing trees was a fear that a coach might need extra copies and I would not have them. My appetite for risk was at absolute zero. In my quest to be indispensable, I couldn't afford to be the guy who hadn't planned for the contingency.

As I walked into the meeting room, Coach Priefer motioned for me to pass the copies out to the players. I finished, sat in the back of the room, and started to take notes. Once the meeting ended, we hit the field, where I set up cones for the day's practice. I was waiting for Prief to acknowledge my brilliant work on the copies, but he was indifferent, barely acknowledging me throughout the day's practice.

As I left the coaches' locker room after my postpractice shower, I got just the kind of thank-you I was after.

"Hey," Priefer said, as he passed me, "stop by my office tonight. I got a project for you."

Mission accomplished. It was happening. I was getting work.

## BREAK IT DOWN

When I knocked on Coach Priefer's office door, he motioned for me to enter without taking his eyes from the television screen. He was watching the kickoff team for the New Orleans Saints. In what seemed like muscle-memory routine, his thumb pressed and re-pressed and re-pressed the rewind button. He was looking for something. I couldn't tell what it was, but from his concentration, it was clear that it was important.

With our third preseason game coming up, we were nearing the most important game for the entire roster. The third preseason match was the game in which starters saw the most playing time. Many coaches viewed this game as a dry run for the season opener.

He slowed the tape down and explained the importance of the project he was about to give me. There were six special teams units on every team: the kickoff and kickoff-return teams, the punt and punt-return teams, and then field goal and field-goal-block units. Coach Priefer wanted me to watch all of the special teams plays for the Saints during the preseason (roughly seventy plays) and to chart which players were used during each play. Because teams needed to evaluate so many players before final cuts, the lineups of the special teams units were constantly changing. We needed to get a handle on who was playing on which units.

Armed with the Saints' roster, a six-pack of Red Bull, and a box of Jolly Ranchers, I began to watch the tape. At first, each play looked like a well-orchestrated NASCAR pileup. High speed. High impact. Bodies flailing everywhere. But after several hours (and broken pencils), my eyes adjusted to the speed and I began to notice the critical pieces of information that I needed—jersey numbers. Now, to the uninitiated, trying to decipher the jersey numbers of players during a football play may seem like a simple task. The process, however, was anything but easy. The pre-high-definition period of video recording made it difficult to identify the jersey numbers of every single player on the field. Given the fact that special teams plays usually span sixty to seventy yards, the tape began to look as if the cameraman was shooting from outer space.

Then there were the nuances of the game that I had not accounted for. The perch from which cameramen recorded games varied from stadium to stadium. Games shot at Gillette Stadium looked great because the shooting distance was just right. A game shot at Soldier Field looked as if a fan on the lower deck were shooting the tape on a handheld camcorder. This was good for viewing the players closest to the camera, but it was a challenge to get a sense of what was happening on the opposite side of the field. And time of day? Sunday afternoon kickoffs could be good or bad. There was usually high visibility for outside games, but the sun's glare could obscure and distort jersey numbers. Number 89 could look like 88, 98, or 68.

And how about conditions? The worst combination of factors was a wet game on a grass field. After a few plays, most jerseys were covered beyond recognition. December posed issues for the teams that played outside, like Green Bay, Chicago, Pittsburgh, and Buffalo. Any visiting team (clad in white jerseys) and covered in snow was a blinding combination. White on white equaled poor visibility.

All of these complexities were challenges that I was completely unprepared to tackle. As I began to review more and more tape, my initial excitement turned into sheer anger. I would be charting plays and would hit a snag where I could not identify one player. As I searched for clues, I began to assemble a troubleshooting list. I would look for identifying markers on certain players. Perhaps a player wore wristbands or tended to wear his socks lower than others. These were important clues to help narrow the pool of suspects.

Skin color also helped. With a picture guide for each team, I could eliminate some candidates for a certain play based on race.

As I began to refine my deductive reasoning, I learned to gather as much information as possible surrounding the events of the game. Injury reports were gold mines. I also ran Google searches for players' names to see if they were mentioned in game recaps.[7] Slowly but surely, I created a detailed troubleshooting list that allowed me to narrow the world of an NFL roster to a small number of potential suspects.

■ ■ ■

This process transcends sector. Regardless of the human resources–generated job description, you must eventually jump feet first into the trenches and figure out everything that wasn't mentioned in your orientation meeting. Sheer persistence is the only way to teach yourself the ins and outs of an organization that are not immediately shared with newcomers.

After three days of film review, I estimated that I had watched film for nearly twenty-four hours. When I turned in my first results, Priefer returned his grading of my work within twelve hours. His Navy pilot–trained eyes were able to catch more of the few details that I had missed.[8] My oversights were circled in red along with the correct answer beside. I felt like I was back in grade school, nervously flipping through a test to see how many questions I had answered incorrectly.

---

7    There is one cliché that is absolutely wrong—"There are no dumb questions." This is untrue. Any Googleable question is better left unasked.

8    Priefer graduated from the U.S. Naval Academy and flew helicopters for Uncle Sam before launching a coaching career.

At the bottom of the final page was a scribbled message: "Go back and look at the tape again. You missed a few guys. Not bad for a rookie.—Prief."

## MY EMPIRE SPREADS TO THE KITCHEN

With an early win under my belt, I continued to scour the building for menial tasks. I quickly found another domain—the kitchen. Our kitchen was an informal dining hall for players. Each weekday they'd stop in to grab breakfast before heading for rehab or position meetings. Their options were of the typical continental breakfast variety: assorted fruit, juices, bread, and cereal. The constant movement of food through our kitchen provided me with an opportunity to grab more responsibility.

On Monday evenings—typically around 6 p.m.—I noticed that our director of football operations, Nate Wainwright, would be busy unpacking groceries in the kitchen. So I made sure to happen into the kitchen at 5:50 every Monday to help him stock the cupboards. To say that Nate was overworked would be an understatement. Not only did he handle all of the head coach's needs, he was also in charge of seemingly every logistical detail, from who sat by whom on the team plane to what dessert would accompany our pregame meal. Taking some of the work off his plate would only help my chances of getting my name on that org chart.

After two weeks of helping, I made my pitch. "I can unload this stuff every week if you want me to. I'm here anyway," I said with a nonchalance that belied my eagerness.

"You sure?" he responded.

"It's no problem. I don't mind. Gives me something to do," I said, playing it off.

"Appreciate that, D," he said, and walked away.

And just like that, my dominion spread from the copy room to the kitchen.

# MONEYBALL MEETS THE GROCERY LIST

After unloading a few shipments, I discovered a few consumption trends. First, I seemed to be throwing out a lot of apples every Monday. Second, the Pop-Tarts with white frosting and sprinkles were always gone by Wednesday morning. And finally, no one drank the two percent milk; this was a whole-milk crowd.

In an era before data analytics had migrated from baseball into football, I was on the front lines of number crunching. I began to keep a weekly tally of what was left over each week. More importantly, I made it a point to overhear comments from the players about what they liked and disliked about our "menu." I felt like a helicopter cook at a *churrascaria*, constantly checking the meat consumption and nervously going back and forth from the kitchen to replenish the options.

After a couple of weeks, I mustered the courage to share my findings with Nate. In the grand scheme of the Chiefs organization, grocery analytics were not a critical concern. Still, I wanted to be respectful of not encroaching on Nate's domain. I was fairly certain that he wouldn't mind if I offered some data-backed advice, but I also didn't want to overstep the boundaries of my position on the staff. Also, would the director of football operations for an NFL team really care what kind of milk the players were drinking?

After showing Nate that we could save about thirty-five bucks a week by shifting some quantities around and elevating some items, he looked up at me with a blank stare. I thought he was going to kick me out of his office.

"Harvard Boy comes through again. I like it. I'll change the order," Nate said.

I had just saved the organization a whopping $140 per month, but I also scored priceless credibility with a key organizational player. As I walked back to my "office," I had a little more bounce to my step. I was getting closer to my destination.

## PIVOT POINTS

1   Map your surroundings—why, how, and what.

2   Identify what others won't (or don't want to) do, then do it.

3   Write the simplest orders with the greatest care.

4   Increase your value by cutting costs.

# CHAPTER 3

# CRASH THE PARTY

## BOTTOM-FEEDING

There are four seasons in the NFL: offseason, preseason, regular season, and postseason. Like the changing of leaves in autumn, there were signs at Arrowhead that we were gradually shifting from the preseason to the regular season.

As we neared our fourth and final preseason game against the St. Louis Rams, the anxiety level in the building spiked. We were still winless. It was apparent we had issues.

Without a clear leader on offense, we embodied the sport's most unforgiving commandment: Thou shalt not win without a good quarterback. We had scored a total of twenty-nine points—that's extremely low output—in three preseason games. Averaging just under ten points per game during the regular season would be disastrous.

In the previous season, the Chiefs had reached the playoffs only to be destroyed by the Indianapolis Colts. None of the coaches or players talked about it. I was learning a major lesson: In the NFL, you are only as good as you are *right now*—and we weren't very good. Wins in the present have more value than wins in the past or the future. It was a crude version of the economic axiom of net present value. In short, going to the playoffs last season didn't amount to squat. We were slated to open the season in Houston on September 9. The clock was ticking.

To accommodate extra players for training camp, the team had installed makeshift lockers earlier in the summer. These rickety contraptions sat on wheels, leaving no question about their temporary status. As we cut players, the temporary lockers were rolled away. Slowly but surely the locker room thinned out, leaving only the permanent lockers bolted to the walls of the room.

Given my tenuous status on the team, I was on edge as the regular season approached. And even though I didn't want to admit it, the one thing that preoccupied my thoughts more than anything else was whether I would travel with the team or not. During the preseason, I had been on each and every flight. But I knew there would be another winnowing of the staff and players into the team's "travel squad." I was nervous, but I realized the best way to displace the anxiety was by working even harder and building my case for indispensability.

Fortunately, my responsibilities were mounting. Prief began asking me to chart the lineups for every upcoming opponent on the schedule. So I started by studying snaps in order to get a good sense of what I was dealing with. Was a kicker left- or right-footed? Did he approach the tee quickly? Was there a tip-off to indicate when a team would run a trick special teams play? Perhaps they broke the huddle quicker than on most snaps? For each of our upcoming opponents, I created a "tendency file." No one told me to do this, but I had a gut feeling that I needed to start building a personal library for every player and coach that we would face.

The NFL is an incestuous league, and coaches as well as players tend to get recycled. While team colors invariably changed after firings and hirings, approaches to the game of football seldom changed dramatically. A coach who had a tendency to call trick plays with one team usually carried the same penchant for chicanery to another team. I wanted to build a data-driven repository of tendencies as well as my impressions of the head coaches, coordinators, and key players that I was likely to face during my career. Along with the data that I collected on each player and coach, I would write my impressions of the player's or coach's philosophy. I kept these notes in a green (color-coded for "money") notebook.

Most people get bogged down in the minutiae of a job. They automatically record the details needed to get through their day. Things like instructions for accessing the company's internal drive and who to call if you need a package delivered are what people tend to focus on. But the more important and valuable points are your impressions of what you see around you. Although I have been allergic to any suggestion that a person keep a "journal," I've realized that is exactly what I was doing and it helped me to navigate a new organization with care and intentionality.

Even when I was inhabiting the bottom of the totem pole and walking through the weeds, I always believed that I would climb the ladder. And without a network of coaches, I was waging a fictional reconnaissance mission. I collected as much information as I could about the major characters in my new world. I approached every assignment I received as if it were the one that would make or break my career.

My attachment to Coach Priefer was natural, but also strategic. Every NFL team has three planets orbiting the head coach: offense, defense, and special teams. In the collective opinion, offense and defense volleyed for the top spot, and special teams tended to bring up the rear. This bias amazed me. Sure, most of the fanfare and highlights of a game involve offensive and defensive plays, but the engine that keeps a team running is special teams. One play—a blocked punt or long kickoff return—could alter the outcome of a game. Nevertheless, special teams were allotted the least amount of time on the practice schedule each week. That reputation caused many of my fellow grunts to put more time and attention into their offensive and defensive duties. They looked at special teams and saw a low-value activity. I looked at special teams and saw a high-value opportunity.

Tackling low-value activities and creating a portfolio of jobs that other people don't want to do is the best way to endear yourself to decision makers and eventually climb the ladder.

In addition to scouting lineups, Coach Priefer gave me another task. I became the unofficial timekeeper for the special teams. As I watched opponent film, I would take a handheld stopwatch and record the time it took from the snap of the ball to when the ball landed in the punter's hands. Then I would time how long it took for the punter to kick the ball after he caught it. Finally, I would chart how long the ball would stay in the air before falling to the field of play.

The first run of times that I turned in were completely wrong. For some reason, I was two- to three-tenths of a second off on most of my times. Priefer said to me, "These are all wrong. All wrong. You're not pulling the trigger on the clock. Pull the trigger!"

Translation: Stop overthinking it. Just go.

In my focus on getting the precise start time, I was delaying the clock start. This process would force me to watch one play more than fifty times before going on to the next play. For all of my meticulous care, I was turning in the wrong answers.

Finally, I stopped stressing about it. I trusted my gut and my eyes and zipped through the tape. The next time I approached Priefer's office, I could feel my hands shaking uncontrollably. As always, he was watching tape, legs up and crossed on his desk. As the images of the screen played across his face, I tiptoed in and placed my notes on a table and turned to creep out.

"Where you going?" Priefer whispered.

"Oh, I just didn't want to bother you. I put the Texans stats on your table."

"Let me see this." He swiveled around and picked up the numbers.

"There we go . . . now we're talking," he said, nodding. "Keep at it. This is good stuff."

"Thanks, Prief," I mumbled as I nearly tripped over my own feet trying to get to the doorway. I rounded the corner, looked both ways, and attempted a jumping side kick. I botched the landing, but I did not care. I was creating value for an NFL coach and was slowly tunneling my foxhole to the front lines of Arrowhead Stadium.

That moment of reassurance from Prief was just what I needed to maintain my momentum. I had been with the team for nearly six weeks; at times I felt like I was sifting through an hourglass and at others I was on a high-speed roller coaster. My body felt as if I had been with the squad for six years. I was slowly acclimating to the four hours of sleep each night, but the rollout phase was dreadful. I'd wake up at 2 a.m. in a panic that I'd missed my alarm and overslept. Or I would dream about racing up the stairs to attend a team meeting, only to see the door close just before I could reach the knob. Another nightmare involved me showing up at practice without my Sharpies. A coach would ask me for a marker and I'd search my pockets before embarrassingly retreating to the background. The disaster of missing an opportunity was at the forefront of my mind, and it was keeping me up at night.

# THE PLANE! THE PLANE![9]

As we approached the first practice of game week, it seemed like everyone wanted to know if I would be traveling with the team.

"Hey, D!" Gunther Cunningham, our defensive coordinator, yelled across the field one day. I ran over to him, expecting an assignment.

9    This is a sly reference to "Ze plane! Ze plane!" which were words uttered by the character Tattoo during every episode of *Fantasy Island*. The show aired during the 1970s and early '80s. Thank me when you win *Jeopardy*.

"Are you going with us to Houston?" he asked.

"I'm not sure, Gun. I haven't heard anything yet. What do you think I should do?"

"Not a damn thing," he said. "Let Herm decide. He's got a lot on his plate right now. Don't bother him and keep doing what you're doing."

"Yep, you're probably right," I agreed and ran back to the other side of the field.

I worked hard to maintain my nonchalance throughout the week. I tried to shrug off the opportunity of a lifetime by acting as if it didn't matter that much to me. There was only one problem: It did matter. It mattered a lot. In fact, traveling with the team was the only thing I could think about. My desire to maintain a "team first" attitude was getting trumped by a desire to work my first *real* NFL game. Being on the sidelines of an NFL game would mean I had really arrived.

The more I tried to gather intel on who would be traveling to Houston for the opener, the more confused I became. I visited the major tribes in the building to see if there was a precedent for someone in my position getting to travel with the team.

First, I stopped by the equipment office—the heart of the NFL circulatory system. Any piece of gear that goes into the administration of an NFL team must be cleared through an equipment office. If you need an extra pair of socks, talk to the equipment guys. If you need extra tackling dummies for a practice drill, talk to the equipment guys. If you need a Chiefs sweater for your mom, talk to the equipment guys.

One benefit of being an equipment guy is that they're typically immune to the inevitable housecleaning that accompanies the firing of coaches every four to five years. New head coaches likely bring in a new slate of assistants, but they rarely make changes to the video and equipment offices. In the government of football, the equipment guys have the closest thing to a lifetime appointment and, thus, the longest institutional memory.

When I walked into the bowels of the equipment office before practice on that pregame Wednesday, the place looked like a disrupted anthill. People were scurrying everywhere. Helmets, Gatorade bottles, chin straps, and shoe boxes were whizzing through the air at a dizzying pace. I ducked a box and pulled up beside one of the equipment guys, Chris Shropshire.

"Hey, do you think I'm gonna get to travel on Saturday?" I asked.

Shrop sized me up. "Do you want me to be honest, or do you want me to blow smoke up your ass?"

"Give it to me straight," I said, bracing myself for not-so-great news.

"Hell, no! Nothing against you, Daron. I just don't see it happening. Are you even on the website?"

He had a point. I wasn't on the website.

"There was a guy like you a few years ago . . . he was a sort of general grunt—no offense—and he never traveled. He just helped us during the week and during home games."

My chances didn't look good, but I wanted a second opinion.

I bounced over to the video department. The video office didn't look much different than the equipment room, with assistants dashing around and packing what appeared to be bulletproof cases with camera equipment in preparation for the day's practice.

"Hey, I got one question. Who thinks I'm going to make the plane for this weekend's game?"

A synchronized laugh filled the room.

"Not a snowball's chance in hell," was the consensus. To put it mildly, my prospects of traveling with the team were looking bleak.

## THE TRASH TROLL

Given the results of my informal poll, the odds were against me. Nevertheless, I needed real, physical evidence to refute the prevailing hypothesis in the building.

I considered several moves. Perhaps I could go through the GM's trash can to see if a draft manifest had been discarded. Visions of being ushered out of Arrowhead in handcuffs had me quickly striking that option from the list.

I could casually scan the GM's desk after hours. As Arrowhead's resident overnighter, I certainly had access. Nope. I envisioned the same outcome.

Finally, I figured it out. The answer was located within my sphere of influence—the copy room. After taking a step back from the situation, I realized there had to be old versions of the flight manifest and seating chart floating around.

A quick glance through the trash can revealed the usual pieces of garbage that can be found with any football team—old rosters, play diagrams, and injury reports. Halfway into the bin and up to my elbows in paper, I got spooked. The revving up of the copy machine had startled me. After making certain that nobody was coming down the hallway, I dove back in.

Up to my nose in rubbish, I finally found what I was looking for—a color-coded sheet of paper.

"Kansas City Chiefs @ Houston Texans. September 8, 2007. Seating Chart."

I felt as if I had just uncovered Hammurabi's Code. I could barely hold the sheet. I was nervous someone would walk in and see me holding it and find me out. I was scared there was a secret camera in the copy room and my actions were being recorded. I was scared I wasn't on the sheet. Simply put, I was a wreck.

As I scanned the sheet, my eyes moved from first class, where the general manager and other team hotshots were seated, to the main cabin, where I saw all of the players I expected. Then, near the back of the plane, were the eight letters that I was searching for.

"D. ROBERTS."

Unable to accept the good news, I racked my brain for a player with the same last name and first initial, only to come up with nothing. I was on the plane! I commenced to perform an impromptu cocktail of the electric slide and running man. With seventy-two hours until takeoff for the Lone Star State, I was ready to start calling my family members in Houston. Luckily, I didn't.

## A CHANGE IS MADE UPSTAIRS

When I laid my head on the trusty Coleman mattress that Wednesday night, I was confident I would be flying the friendly skies with the Chiefs to Houston. I went to bed thinking of the chills I would feel when hearing the national anthem. I saw visions of myself wearing a Motorola headset, roaming the sideline.

The rhythm of Thursday went as usual. Coaches met with other coaches. Coaches met with players. Players practiced. And then we all did it again. At the end of the evening, Nate Wainwright asked me to pass out the itinerary and seating charts to everyone in the organization. As he handed me the stack, he smiled. "You made the plane, Rook."

"I did?" I grinned. "That's awesome."

"Now, make enough copies and pass them out," Nate barked. I scurried to the copy room.

As I went from office to office dropping the itineraries on deserted desks and sliding them under closed doors, I felt like I had beat the house in a game of high-stakes poker. I was riding high on a wave of victory. And looking back on my reaction, I can admit that I let myself reach a level of comfort that I had promised myself I would never do. That night, I sent emails to my parents with the subject line, "I MADE THE PLANE!!!"

And then, with one fell swoop, my bubble burst.

I knew something was wrong as soon as I walked into Nate's office.

"Sorry, man. We had to make a few changes to the flight. You're not going to travel with us this weekend. Maybe next time."

As he handed a copy of the updated seating chart to me, he asked, "Can you make copies and pass them around?"

Not only had I been kicked off the plane, but I had to deliver a hundred copies of my death certificate to everybody in the building. Just to make sure Nate wasn't playing the worst prank in the history of organized sports, I scrutinized the sheet. I held it up to the light; I flipped it over. I did that again, and then again. Perhaps I was overlooking my name. But the reality began to set in. With so many names and color-coded blocks, I couldn't figure out if I had been replaced by someone else or merely chopped from the list.

I placed the sheet in the copier, punched in 100, and pressed Start.

As the copier jolted through its job, I scanned every event, every interaction, and every task since I had started working in July. I couldn't point to a single episode that would justify my removal from the plane.

*I knew I shouldn't have laughed at that joke,* I thought. Or, *maybe I didn't set up the cones the right way?*

For the life of me, I couldn't figure out what I had done or not done. A wave of self-doubt washed over me.

The screech of the copier shook me from my retrospection. I gathered the copies and walked out.

As I passed out the amended seating charts, the reaction ranged from unaffected to shocked.

"What in the hell did you do, D?" Gun asked after looking at the updated sheet.

"Nothing. Yesterday I was on the plane, and today I'm off."

"Sounds like the GM axed you. Must be a money issue."

I hung on the last two words like a rock climber fighting for his life: money issue. That was it—it wasn't personal. Maybe my change in status had absolutely nothing to do with me. I was just another variable pushing up the total cost for the organization.

No matter the reason, there was no time for sulking. It was time to craft my plan of attack. But first, I needed more information.

I went back to Nate's office. In the football universe, the director of football ops is akin to a chief of staff. All logistical roads lead to this point on the organizational chart.

Nate was dodgy. This surprised me because I didn't know him

as a dodgy type of guy. He normally relayed information with the matter-of-factness of an investment banker. Now, he was speaking in platitudes and keeping a safe orbit around the issue with his language. Finally, I asked him directly, "Was this decision made by the GM?" He nodded.

"You think it's a cost issue?" I asked.

"What do you think, Harvard Boy?"

The guessing game was over. I quickly began to assess my options:

Option A: Do nothing and watch the game from a bar.

Option B: Confront the general manager.

Option C: Ask Herm to make an intercession on my behalf.

Option D: Fly to Houston on my own dime and crash the party.

Well, I wasn't going for Option A. I had sacrificed too much to watch this game from some dive bar in Kansas City. The lack of a relationship with the GM disqualified Option B. Although I had spoken to him on a few occasions, I didn't have a real connection with him.

I had two choices: Option C or Option D. Go to Herm or go to Orbitz.

My account of goodwill was in the black with Herm, but I wanted to keep it that way. I already had plans to ask him for a full-time position at the end of the year, so I needed to save my chips for that moment. And just like that, I was left with only one choice: Option D.

I ran back to my impromptu office and jumped on my computer. A quick online search revealed that Southwest would be my cheapest option. I was forty-eight hours from kickoff. I called the Southwest customer service line and bought a cheap ticket from Kansas City to Houston.

But how would I get around Houston? Fortunately, I had several cousins living in the state's most populated city. Perhaps I could ask one of them to give me a ride? But after charting all of the trips I would have to take, I realized it would be risky to rely on others to navigate through Houston traffic. If I missed a meeting, I wanted only one person to blame—me. So I rented the cheapest car, booked the cheapest hotel, and started drafting my own itinerary. I was going rogue.

## OPERATION HOUSTON

The Saturday before a Sunday matchup is the last chance for NFL teams to prepare for Sunday's game. It's a light physical day for the players—no shoulder pads or helmets—but a mentally taxing day for everyone. Every contingency is considered. If this player goes down with an injury in the first quarter, who will replace him? If we are unable to move the ball on offense by running our usual power plays, how will we adjust? This incessant process of talking and walking through contingencies of a game is an incredible experience, not to be missed. Players must get on the same page with coaches. Coaches must get on the same page with players. And the head coach orchestrates the entire process with the precision of a surgeon.

As soon as our meetings and walk-throughs wrapped up, the coaches and players showered up and prepared for the drive to the airport.

My plan was simple. I would hang back until the last coach left the building, then I would get dressed and drive to the airport. My flight would give me roughly an hour to check in at my hotel and drive downtown to attend 7 p.m. meetings.

As I packed, I was intent upon keeping the process simple, but I prepared for every contingency. I packed three boxes of Sharpies (red, black, and blue), two boxes of mechanical pencils, and three boxes of pens (red, black, and blue). I stashed two stopwatches and three notepads and I closed my suitcase.

As I exited the stadium, I realized I had forgotten the most important item I would need for the weekend. I ran into the kitchen and grabbed a plastic table covering. It was your typical picnic pattern, adorned with red and white squares. I was certain that I would need it for the bed in my hotel room—the online photos of my $29.99 bargain were frightening to say the least. I was on my way.

In Houston, I rushed through Hobby Airport to the car rental center. My cheap car was located at an off-site location, adding an unexpected delay to my itinerary. With a tight turnaround, I decided to nix the hotel check-in. I changed into my suit in the car, nervously knotted my tie, and zoomed downtown.

As I walked through the sliding doors of the team hotel, my heart was pounding loud enough to be heard by anyone in the lobby. I had visions of being escorted out of the building by the security guards monitoring the team meeting areas.

Clutching my team itinerary, I rode the escalator to the floor of the meeting rooms. Just as I suspected, a security guard greeted me.

"Can I help you?" he asked.

"Uh, yes . . . I'm a defensive assistant with the team."

The guard looked at me.

"Team ID?" he asked.

As I fumbled for my wallet, which *did not* contain a team ID

(I didn't have an ID; I wasn't technically on the team), one of our video managers walked by.

"Hey, D."

"Hey, man!" I started to follow him and hoped the security guard wouldn't stop me. He didn't. I was in.

As I walked into the special teams meeting, the room was dark and quiet. Coach Priefer was preparing his meeting slides and players were mumbling to each other.

I sat in the back, took out my notebook, and tried to act as if I was supposed to be there.

A couple of players patted me on the shoulder as they walked toward the front. When Nate saw me, he did a double take and mouthed, "You crazy sonofabitch."

I nodded and waited for the meeting to begin.

After the initial meeting, we broke into offensive and defensive units and then capped the night with a team meeting led by Coach Edwards. This was it. It felt as if we were sitting in a pre-mission Navy SEAL briefing. None of my preseason prep meetings could compare to what I was witnessing. The preseason was a practice run. Now the score really mattered and the air in the room reeked of anticipation.

Coach Edwards's talk was short and to the point. Do your job tomorrow. Don't worry about anyone else's job but your own. If we all do our jobs we will win. Period.

I'm sure Coach Edwards was surprised to see me at the end of the meeting, but he played it off with his characteristic Northern California cool smirk. Nate handed a game-day credential to me that I would need the next day. Looking back, I don't know what I would have done had Herm told me to leave. Well, actually, I would have hustled out. But in the moment, I never considered it to be an option. As I had packed my bags in Kansas City, I had one image in my mind—walking the sidelines of Reliant Stadium during Sunday's game. I had manifested a new reality and I was ready to claim it.

"If you can get to the visitor's loading dock, show this credential and it will get you into the locker room," Nate said, almost like it was a dare.

I thanked him, jumped into my Toyota Corolla, and began the thirty-minute drive to my budget motel. I had done it! I hadn't been arrested or carried out of the building by security. I made it over the first hurdle. Now it was time to get ready for the game.

As I opened the door to my hotel room, I was hit in the face with the stink of decades of Virginia Slims smokers. The room looked like it hadn't changed in thirty years. I took out my picnic table cover, threw it over the top of the bed, set three alarms, scheduled two wake-up calls, and tried to sleep.

It didn't work. I tossed and turned. I was deathly afraid to close my eyes despite the safety net I had in five alarms. Although kickoff was at noon, I was consumed with the fear of missing it.

I was willing to risk some resentment from my peers for crashing the party, bewilderment from my head coach, and $300 to double-down on my dream of becoming a head coach. Getting to the first game of the season was my Rubicon moment. Playing it safe is standing on the shore, dry and comfortable. Doubling down on your dreams is a tough crossing. It doesn't feel good and you will certainly get soaked. There's a queasiness tinged with fear that will drive you mad. But if you think being great is difficult, try being mediocre.

## PIVOT POINTS

1   Create "tendency files" on your competition. Understand why and when they do what they do.

2   Convert low-value activities into high-value opportunities.

3   Stay even. Don't get too high, don't dip too low, and don't show your disappointment.

4   Circumvent the system when the system circumvents you.

# CHAPTER 4

# FAKE IT 'TIL THEY TAKE IT

Although I wanted to get eight hours of sleep before the game, I knew it would be next to impossible. First, the room smelled like an ashtray. Second, a never-ending cascade of dreams and nightmares jolted me at regular intervals throughout the night.

The most horrifying episode involved Coach Edwards turning to me with two seconds left on the clock. We were down by seven points and had one last play to score a touchdown. Out of nowhere, Herm grabbed my arm and said, "What play should we run?" In the dream, I could feel his hand crushing my flesh against bone. He yelled, "Daron, are you listening to me, what play should we run?"

I woke up in a cold sweat, mumbling, "But I'm not even on offense. I'm not on offense . . . I'm not on offense."

In another nightmare, I was standing on the sideline and watching the game unfold when I noticed the Texans players were walking toward me after finishing a series. (A series is the group of continuous plays that a football unit—offense, defense, or special teams—runs during a game.) That was odd, I thought. Then I looked to my left and right. I was surrounded by Texans personnel. My heart leapt into overdrive and my body temperature spiked. I was on the wrong sideline. I must have taken a right, when I should have taken a left as I exited the locker room at halftime. My embarrassment gave way to shock and quickly became panic. How could I get back to the Chiefs' sideline discreetly? There had to be some way for me to sneak behind the end zone and reach my team. At just that moment, the taunts erupted from the hecklers in the stands. "Hey, what the hell are you doing, Chief Boy? Get your ass back on the other side of the field!"

It was at this moment that I jolted awake. Drenched in sweat, I flipped on the lamp and checked my satchel for the following day's necessary tools. After the tenth check, I convinced myself that I had everything I needed. I was prepared. Still, that assurance wasn't enough to stamp down the self-doubt and fear that kept creeping to the surface.

I clearly wasn't going to get any meaningful sleep, so I opened my green notebook and started to write. I was nervous, I was scared, and I was excited. I had to get my thoughts on paper:

*September 9, 2007*

*Dear Daron,*

*It's 3:12 a.m. and you're sitting in the dirtiest motel in Houston, Texas. Tomorrow will be your first NFL game. You made it through training camp, you made it through the preseason, and tomorrow is when it counts. You have traveled a long way from the safe confines of Cambridge. Law school was hard, but at least it was predictable. Mort the Tort, the smell of Gropius dorm, those were all constants in the equation of your past three years.*

*This is different. Most of the time you feel out of place and invisible. People walk by you in the hallways and barely nod. You're tired.*

*Ten years from now, the goal is to be a head coach in the NFL. Don't forget that. Jon Gruden did it.*[10]

*What You Need to Do Tomorrow:*
1. *Breathe.*
2. *Smile (but not too much).*
3. *Stay out of the way (but be close enough to be noticed).*
4. *Be useful. (DON'T BE A FAN. Coach hates that.)*
5. *Have fun.*

The detachment of writing as an observer allowed me to step outside of myself, if only for a few minutes. During my travels across

---

10    After getting unceremoniously fired as head coach of the Tampa Bay Buccaneers in 2009, Gruden formed the Fired Football Coaches Association (FFCA). It is unclear what the association actually does.

the world, I always kept detailed journals. Upon rereading them, I was amazed at how consumed I was by the moment. I was almost too focused on my own experiences to offer any advice to the future me. The lost love in Barcelona, the fear at the Cambodian border because my passport was "stamped out." Using "I" and "me" felt cathartic in those moments, and I wanted this pregame writing to be a useful guide to me as a coach down the road. I decided to keep the emotion in my writing, but also add some instructive nuggets I could use as I prepared to coach in Super Bowl LXI.

In my early morning reflection, I recalled a pivotal moment in my journey to the NFL: watching Tony Dungy and Lovie Smith square off in Super Bowl XLI. My roommate and I hosted a game-watching party at our apartment. Everyone at the party knew where they would land after graduation, but I was still waiting for the phone to ring. As the people in our apartment sipped cheap wine, grazed on Costco party platters, and chatted about their future law firms, I focused on the game. Playing out before my eyes were two friends (Smith had coached for Dungy in Tampa Bay) trading jabs across a football field. Their coexistence in this game was a testament that a coach could treat his players with respect, push them to be good men beyond the game, and still rise to the top. It was also the first time a championship game featured any African-American head coach, let alone head coaches at the helms of both teams.

Dungy was a man who was famous for rarely raising his voice during a game or practice. In a profession rife with overzealous yellers, he stood out as a true "player's coach," finding the difficult balance between humility and respect. His players respected him because he respected them. Dungy was an unapologetic man of faith, and his book *Quiet Strength* would secure his perch as the sport's moral compass. As a Dungy coaching offspring, Lovie Smith carried a similar approach with him to the Chicago Bears.

Watching these two men battle, I knew that was where I wanted to be: on the sidelines of sport's biggest duel. As the game drew to an end and Dungy hoisted the Lombardi Trophy, I closed my eyes and imagined it was me. I couldn't remember the last time a television scene created such an aspirational moment for me. But imagining myself in that moment was not enough; I wanted to be there.

Now, as the clock advanced toward the noon kickoff in my first NFL game, my moment of reverie flipped into intense fear. I don't mean that clichéd horror-movie feeling in the pit of my stomach sort of fear. No, this variety pressed the accelerator on my heart. It was beating against my chest. It was vibrating in my ear canal. An endless cascade of things that could go wrong raged in my head. I didn't have the right color of slacks to wear (I brought every shade in Haggar's collection). NFL security would not let me into the visitor's locker room. A bomb-sniffing dog would detect some substance in my suitcase and the ensuing episode would not only keep me out of the stadium, it would send me to the top of the terrorist watch list. I was a nervous wreck.

I tried to redirect my energy to recalling all the research I had done the previous week. Nervous about the Reliant Stadium policy on bags, I had called the ticket office and taken detailed notes on the proper size of permitted bags and prohibited items. Nervous about the color of slacks that coaches would wear, I pulled the TV copy of the previous season's seventeen games (including the first-round playoff debacle) and scanned the sidelines. With catlike precision, I would stab the Pause button on my remote and zoom in. Seventeen games, thirteen opponents, one color of pants: light brown.

In a world of uncertainty, where my status was constantly being reevaluated, I had sucked as much "unknowingness" out of the equation as I possibly could. In my moment of pregame panic, I had to remind myself that I was prepared. Obsession. Overpreparation. Obsessive-compulsive disorder. Call it what you will. I had done everything in my power to control every variable I could.

## THE MISSION

By my calculation, I had to leave for the stadium at 7:30 a.m. It would take me twenty-two minutes to drive from the hotel to Reliant. Because I didn't have a parking pass, I would need to find an affordable spot that was still in the same time zone as the stadium.

Since I needed to leave at 7:30 a.m., I decided to leave at 6:45 a.m. My general philosophy is to take a "negative" mindset in only one instance—time calculation. In general, I am a very positive person, but when planning to get to practice, or in this case my first game, I assumed the worst. What if I get a flat tire? What if I get pulled over by the cops? What if I get pulled over by the cops and they take me in for questioning because they pop the trunk of my rental car and lift the carpeting and find a kilo of cocaine that was left behind by the last driver? The infinite world of bad things that could happen occupied my mind. This resulted in an equation for arriving at places far in advance of any reasonable person.[11]

---

11    This practice guides my approach to meetings. The good nuggets of a meeting usually happen before everyone arrives (and while a few decision makers are in the room) or right after the meeting (when the decision makers have left and the lower-level employees are reviewing what was decided).

Because my motel was not the kind of place to offer a delightful continental breakfast spread, I got out of there with little delay. I refused to use the tap water to brush my teeth or shower, so I snagged a couple of bottled waters from the hotel and grabbed my trusty Drysol antiperspirant to perform my ablutions. So, with my underarms smelling relatively good and my clothes smelling like an ashtray, I closed the door to my room, descended the stairs, and jumped into my rental. It was time to head to Reliant.

# KEEP WALKING

The tailgating scene at Reliant was more exciting than I expected. While it didn't rival the parking lot revelry of a Southeastern Conference matchup, there were enough Jack Daniel's bottles and Lone Star cans littering the ground to indicate that fans had sufficiently christened the opening game. As I circled the stadium, I surveyed my parking options and made strategic calculations about getting to the airport.

The game would end at approximately 3:45 p.m., assuming we didn't go into overtime. The last thing that I needed was to get trapped in the bumper-to-bumper exodus from Reliant, so I decided to find private parking on the periphery of the stadium with the hope that I could bolt from the locker room right after the game and hit the highway with minimal interference.

I pulled into a lot guarded by a guy frantically waving a red flag. Actually, it wasn't really a parking lot as much as it was an abandoned plot of land that only functioned as a cash cow when there were events at Reliant. I slowly navigated around the massive potholes, trying to avoid damaging the rental car that had to be returned in twelve hours.

As I emerged from the car, the parking attendant looked me up and down and said, "Twenty bucks, big dog."

Looking me over, he continued: "You work game days?"

"Huh?" I mumbled, preoccupied by my concern that I couldn't find the twenty-dollar bill I had stashed for parking. As I plumbed every pocket on my body, I could feel the parking attendant doing a full body scan.

"Tell the truth, man. You work at the stadium? You a sportswriter? I ain't never seen nobody take a briefcase to a football game."

As I finally located the twenty, I took a minute to consider what he was seeing in my appearance. I was wearing a gray suit, white shirt, and red tie. I had a small briefcase and a roller bag. The briefcase contained everything that I would need for the game; the roller bag had every piece of contingency clothing that I might need for the game.

As I handed him the bill and deflected his line of inquiry, a group of college-aged kids walked by clad in Texans-colored Mardi Gras beads, red cups in hand.

Yep, I was out of place. No wonder the guy was suspicious.

I walked across the street and headed for the stadium. Nate's words from the previous night echoed in my brain.

"D, don't think twice. This pass is going to get you anywhere you need in the stadium. Just act like you're supposed to be there. Don't be fidgety. Don't hesitate. Flash the pass and keep it moving," Nate advised. In hindsight, it was good general advice, too.

Clearly, he had not considered the litany of worst possible scenarios that were endlessly running through my mind. As an NFL veteran, Nate had been to every NFL stadium and had navigated endless airports and locker rooms with ease. But I was as nervous as a college free agent the night before final cuts.

As I started running across the parking lot of Reliant, I noticed my clothes felt uncomfortable. My shirt was drenched and it was starting to show on my suit jacket. I heard Herm's voice in my head: "Put yourself in a position to win." But If I walked up to a security guard and flashed my all-access pass looking as if I had just finished the Boston Marathon, I would not be putting myself in the best position to win. Herm had been talking about a tight end trying to block a defensive end and a wide receiver going up for a ball in the end zone, but he was also talking to me in the blue lot of Reliant Stadium. I needed to apply his advice to the most important play for me of the day: getting into the stadium.

The behemoth of Reliant steadily grew in size as I got closer to the stadium. I found my gate and did a casual walk-by to get a quick reconnaissance of the location. As I'd guessed, the scene didn't look much different than what I had seen in the preseason. There were security guards, easily detectable in their yellow-and-black shirts with walkie-talkies strapped to their sides and microphones hung over their shoulders. There were also Houston Police Department officers, with their bomb-sniffing dogs leading their handlers around buses and over equipment boxes.

I took a deep breath and considered what was in front of me: organized chaos. Security was engaged in keeping everyone safe. The groundskeepers were worried about the quality of the field. The stadium attendants were concerned with the cleanliness of the stands. I was the least of their concerns.

As I neared the first security guard, I scanned my mental checklist.

1   Make eye contact.

2   Smile.

3   Nod.

4   Keep it moving.

I approached the security officer. I looked him right in the eyes, smiled, and motioned to the pass attached to my belt loop.

Every sound and sight around me morphed into an indistinguishable mass and all I could see were the peering eyes of the security guard. He looked down at the pass, looked back at me, and nodded. I was in.

Descending the ramp into the bowels of Reliant, I began to see Chiefs personnel and I knew I was in friendly territory. Equipment managers were rolling large bins of socks, jocks, T-shirts, and headbands around at a frenetic pace. Officials huddled together, game-day personnel herded VIP guests for the pregame show, and players walked onto the field and began their pregame rituals. I made my way through the chaos and found the locker room.

"D! You made it," Nate shouted.

As Herm's right-hand man, he had his finger on the pulse of the entire operation. What looked like pandemonium to me was actually an orchestrated operation crafted, scheduled, and managed by Nate. Roaming the halls of the locker room and incessantly checking his watch, Nate was on the lookout for any event that was transpiring ahead or behind schedule. He was the first to see me.

The look he gave me let me know that he was somewhat surprised that I made it into the holiest of holy lands.

"How was the shitty hotel?" Nate asked.

"Fine." I shrugged it off. "I was knocked out as soon as I got back. Any major hiccups last night?"

"Nope. We ate. Did bed check, and that was it."

As I meandered through the ever-moving collision course, I walked by the eerily silent coaches' locker room. Coaches were reviewing their game plans and finishing up last-minute preparations. Although I didn't expect to have my own locker, I was somewhat hopeful that I might find a corner to change my clothes. Nope. The space was too tight and I didn't want to ask the coaches if I could squeeze by them.

I walked into the equipment room and grabbed the first person I could find.

"Hey, can I please get a game-day shirt?"

"We got you covered, come over here."

As Shrop slowly opened the trunk, it seemed as if a fuzzy, warm, yellow glow emanated from within.[12] Game-day gear was unlike any other apparel that we wore during the year. Each game had a unique uniform variation designed by Reebok. In any given season there was an assortment of game-day varieties: cancer awareness month, Veteran's Day, and old-school throwback gear were just a few. For today's game, there were four different variations of Chiefs tops, two different options for shoes, and a host of other items that I didn't even know existed.

"Man, you guys bring a lot of stuff on the road," I marveled.

"Rule number one, D: Never get caught with your pants down. The one thing we can't do is jump on a plane back to KC to pick up

---

12    It felt as if Shrop was opening the *Pulp Fiction* briefcase.

some gear on the day of a game. So we pack up everything and more than we could possibly need on a road trip."

"Man," I said as I stared in awe.

"D, I love you, man, but I got some more important guys to take care of. Can you hurry up and grab a shirt so I can get to them?" he asked.

"Thanks, man, I owe you one."

I found a vacant corner and changed my clothes in record time. I had even brought a plastic hook to create a makeshift closet for myself. I stuck it to the wall, hung up my suit and shirt, and made my way to the field.

## A GAME OF RITUALS

As I walked through the tunnel, the stadium lights grew brighter as I neared field level. I had arrived.

This was definitely not the preseason. Sportswriters and newscasters were scattered around the field. VIP fans for both teams were snapping pictures and waiting for a sighting of their favorite players—enjoying the total pregame treatment.

What struck me as I looked across the field was the variety of pregame warm-ups unfolding before my eyes. Close to the fifty-yard line, a group of running backs were stretching together. In the corner of an end zone, a few defensive backs were working on backpedaling drills. Their progression went from forty-five-degree turns to ninety-degree turns. Then they practiced man turns and zone turns. Rapid foot-fire drills were next. Most of the players had large headphones protruding from their ears, and their heads bobbed to some beat as the ringleader motioned for a new drill to start. Words were unnecessary—each team had its own sign language.

I was brought out of my reverie when the kickers and long snappers emerged from the tunnel. Their outlines alerted me to the one thing that I failed to bring with me to the field—a stopwatch. I couldn't remember if I had packed the stopwatch or not and this uncertainty sent my momentarily calm heart rate back through the roof. I would absolutely need a stopwatch to record the timing of our specialists.

I started to backpedal with the stealth of a veteran cornerback. Once I was twenty yards from the group, I turned. With the speed of an overweight law school grad, I sprinted back to the locker room and attacked my suitcase. Finally, I found what I was looking for— the backup (to the backup) stopwatch that I had stashed in a small compartment of my briefcase. With a tremendous sigh of relief, I snatched the watch and ran back to the field.

As I made it to Coach Priefer's huddle, Jean-Philippe Darche snickered and gave me a look that said he knew exactly what had happened. As soon as the huddle broke, he walked over and whispered, "Looks like Harvard Boy forgot his stopwatch. Don't worry, I won't tell Prief."

My heart sank. I thought I had departed the field without being detected by anyone. Obviously, I hadn't been as stealthy as I thought. It was probably that poorly executed backpedal and pivot.

I took out my notebook and went to work recording the hang times and distances of each of our kicks. I also noted an approximate location on the field of where the kicks fell. The goal was to get a good sense of how our specialists were operating on game day. Adrenaline and anxiety created a lethal combination and could wreak havoc on normal tendencies. The special teams coach had to understand how his specialists were operating before kickoff because the coach was in constant communication with the head coach during the course of a game.

Should we punt on third down? Was the distance too far to take a shot at a field goal? Was it time for us to run a fake punt? All of these questions would arise at some point during the course of the game, and given the time sensitivity of the matchup, the head coach would need an answer within seconds. There was no time for a long-winded debate. My pregame observations would help to inform Prief's decisions.

The challenging aspect of my pregame responsibility was to record our data while also recording the same information for our opponent. I had to keep one eye on the Texans' kicker at all times. After observing a few kicks, it was clear to me that he was having a good day. He achieved good hang time and was dropping shots with precision.[13] It was clear that we would have our work cut out for us that day.

Once the specialists finished kicking practice, offensive and defensive position groups began to emerge from the tunnel. The meticulously orchestrated schedule was executed without a hiccup.

Within a matter of minutes, players from both teams peppered each half of the field. The symbolic barrier of the fifty-yard line

---

13    The longer it takes for a kick to land in the field of play, the more time defenders have to travel to the returner. This is a good thing. A shorter hang time means two factors are usually at play—a shorter distance of the kick, and less time for your defenders to get to the returner. This is a recipe for disaster, as we would find out the next week when we faced Devin Hester.

separated them as they stretched and moved into position drills. Coach David Gibbs—Gibby—pulled the defensive backs together and calmly said, "Let's get to work." And with that, we sped through our practice drills at breakneck speed. Guys were jumping around, feeling good and ready to roll into the first game of the season.

Once pregame warm-ups were done, we reconvened in the locker room, where the full spectrum of human emotions was on display. Seasoned veterans were sitting calmly at their lockers. A rookie was throwing up in the bathroom. A couple of offensive linemen were shoving each other. Although I had witnessed this moment in the pre-season, there was a very different feeling in the air. We were twelve minutes from the beginning of a grueling, sixteen-game gauntlet.

## STAY READY SO YOU WON'T HAVE TO GET READY

At kickoff, it was clear that we were in for a dogfight. The 2007 Texans were a talented team and the home crowd was energized for the opener. I was determined to stay no more (and no fewer) than three steps behind Coach Priefer as he followed the action of the game. As a special teams coordinator, his finger never left the pulse of the team. He was attuned to every aspect of the game and was ready to summon his support squad if the situation called for it. But while the offensive and defensive staffs were teeming with extra help, Prief coached the most players on the team *by himself*. I was going to show him that I was the right-hand man he never knew he needed. He was anxious to let me help him wrangle the players who would shuttle back and forth from the field to the sidelines. And in Prief fashion, he shoved the depth charts into my hands, gave me a nod, and kept walking.

One of my most important jobs was "running pictures" after each series—essentially, I was the king of the sideline copier. After a series was completed, an antiquated printer would labor to emit two diagrams of each play—the sideline and end zone copies. The sideline copy was a reliable picture of all twenty-two players. Most good coaches could catch seventy-five percent of the activity on a given play. But for some plays, the mass of twenty-two players moving at a high rate of speed created enough confusion to warrant an investigation. So, for each play, a coach needed to put the pieces together to see what actually transpired on a given play.[14]

At the end of each special teams play, I'd collect the pictures from the printer, throw them in a three-ring binder, and organize them by play. This was one of the toughest game-day jobs. I offered to do the job because no one else really wanted it. Essentially, you're the game-day bearer of bad news. When there is a good play, the coach says nothing to the deliverer of the printouts. But when there is a bad play (and for a team not playing well, there are a lot of bad plays), the deliverer of printouts usually receives a "What the fuck happened?" or "Let me see those" accompanied with a vicious snatch from the

---

14    The sources of feedback for any given play fell into one of three categories: player input, coach assessment, and computer printouts. A player's performance on a play could sometimes color his assessment of what transpired. Oftentimes, coaches would accept a player's version only to find out later that the player was completely wrong. While coaches' assessments tended to be more accurate, they might fall victim to confirmation bias. They could picture the way a particular play had been drawn on the whiteboard and programmed in the computer. But, as Herm liked to say, the only problem with football is that "the X's and O's tend to move." In other words, offensive and defensive schemes could look great on paper, but the eleven men on the line of scrimmage and the play-calling of the opposing coach created a perfect medley of unpredictability.

coach. As I heard veteran interns talk about the stress that was involved with transporting printouts, I knew I had to have the job.

For a split second, I wondered if asking for the task would amount to overreaching, but as the man even lower than the low man on the totem pole, there really was no such thing. If you want to advance, whether you're a rookie journalist or budding photographer, you must overreach. Asking for the difficult tasks that most people loathe must be an automatic response to any situation. The lunacy of asking for the worst jobs in an office will only build your mythology and establish your credibility.

As I waited for the pictures to finish, I would glance nervously at Coach Priefer. Then I'd look back at the printer. Then back to Priefer. He'd give me a look that screamed, "Where are my damn pictures?" I'd grab the book, then zigzag through the crowded sideline to get the pictures to Prief.

We hadn't yet reached halftime, but it was clear that this game was not going the way we had planned. Special teams plays imploded with each snap. Justin Medlock, our rookie kicker from UCLA, missed what should have been an automatic kick for us at a distance of thirty yards. It was only the first quarter, but in a league where the margin of victory is so small, every possession counted. As Medlock approached the sideline, Prief asked, "What was the problem?" Justin just shrugged and kept walking. In practice, he had nailed kicks like this as warm-up shots. But with the pressure of opening day, he was a different man. As I watched him walk over to the bench, it was clear to me that this could be the beginning of something very bad for us. A rookie losing confidence early—especially a kicker—was a sure sign of tanking or, worse yet, getting cut.

In the second quarter, the debacle continued. Eddie Drummond, an experienced veteran returner we had picked up from the Detroit Lions, fumbled a punt. The Texans recovered it. As the play unfolded, all I could hear was, "You gotta be kidding me!" We were two quarters into our first game of the season, and special teams were responsible for two major mishaps. Prief yelled at me to bring him the pictures. As he examined the documents, he said, "You gotta be kidding me . . . you gotta be kidding me."

The day was a complete disaster for the whole team. Without a touchdown to our credit, we walked off the field after taking a bona fide shellacking. Final score: 20–3, bad guys win.

As players took a knee on the locker room floor, the silence was deafening. Herm kept it simple: "We are a better team than what we showed out there today. We made it easy for those guys. In this league, if you don't tackle and you give the ball away, you will never have a chance to win. Let's come in tomorrow, watch the tape, and get the mistakes corrected. When you guys come back in on Wednesday, we will move on to the Bears. I can promise you this, the Bears won't feel sorry for you. Let's get our minds right."

As I drove to the airport, I thought through all I had seen over the course of the last twenty-four hours. I also thought about how easy it could have been for me to have viewed this game from a bar in Kansas City. But I wanted more. I decided to blend into the fabric of the team so it would become more difficult to get rid of me.

In my quest for indispensability, I became the ultimate party crasher. Although I had a few allies on the team, many people remained skeptical of my intentions. I needed to be that constant, quasi-annoying force that was eager to do any task, anytime, anywhere. That was my ultimate goal.

That laser-like focus should be the main driver for not only anyone trying to break into a new environment, but for those wanting to *stay* there. Other interns who had worked for the team during training camp were content to accept that they had not been hired and to return home with a few good stories and some Chiefs gear. Not me. I wanted more. You should, too.

## PIVOT POINTS

1 Remove as much "unknowingness" from the equation as possible.

2 Put yourself in a position to win.

3 If you want to advance, you must overreach. Become the ultimate party crasher.

4 Visualize how your dream will unfold. Don't get discouraged if the script changes.

# CHAPTER 5

# SET YOURSELF APART BY DRESSING THE PART

"Welcome to Kansas City. Thank you for flying with Southwest Airlines." The voice of the flight attendant jolted me awake. It was late, and I needed to get to the office. Although our loss against the Texans was less than six hours old, I knew there would be no rest for the weary. The focus would shift to the Chicago Bears, and the Bears were a talented team. We had barely won our preseason game against them 20–19. The 2006 NFC champions were fresh off a Super Bowl defeat and were looking for a second chance to make a return trip to the big game.

The Bears' first test of the 2007 season was against the San Diego Chargers, our division rivals. As I walked through the terminal at MCI airport, I stopped to check the score updates:

Minnesota 24, Atlanta 3

Carolina 27, St. Louis 13

Denver 15, Buffalo 14

San Diego 14, Chicago 3

I stopped in my tracks. I wasn't expecting to see that score.

I wanted to see the game film as soon as possible. Watching the Bears-versus-Chargers game would be a two-for-one deal, since we were scheduled to play San Diego twice in the 2007–2008 season. I sped from the airport to the stadium. Even though it was late, there were a few support staffers hanging around the office. When the coaches arrived at 4:30 a.m. the next morning, they would expect the previous day's game to be queued up and ready to watch. Although I was anxious to start watching the Bears game, I paused.

What was important now? The most important thing right now was to learn from the Texans game. I started a pot of coffee and went down to the locker room. After taking a hot shower and nabbing a few Red Bulls, I ascended the stairs and poured a cup of coffee. It was time to get to work.

# POSTMORTEM

I decided the most important task was to identify what went wrong in each play. Herm stressed the need to identify whether a poor play was a result of player error (that is, a player not fulfilling his responsibilities on the play) or coach error (a coach putting players in a bad position by calling the wrong play).

First, I had to review the game. For each play, there was a list of several variables to provide context to the event. What was the down and distance? The quarter? Time remaining on the clock? Field position? Score? All of these questions informed why a particular play was called.

Next, I needed to populate the eleven-player rows on my spreadsheet. The player's jersey number would go in the first column of the spreadsheet. After that loomed a column with a fairly benign title: "Comments." Those cells would contain the critical info that could create, continue, or kill a player's professional career. Coaches used the postgame analysis to make a final assessment of how a player performed every single play of the season. In addition to the coach, copies of the report were given to the player and the general manager. While the coaching side of the building handled the game-to-game decisions associated with a team's performance, the GM spearheaded the trades, acquisitions, and cuts.

Now, I was going to grade each special teams player's performance from the opening game. I would fill out the exact sheet that Coach Priefer would complete and then compare his notes to my observations. Since I had attended every meeting that Prief had led since the beginning of the season, I knew what he expected of all of the players. Now, I would try to match the tape with my own knowledge and hone my assessment skills. Just as the players would receive a final grade for their performance, I would grade my own.

As Coach Edwards would say, "The eye in the sky don't lie." Translation: The film could be trusted above everything else. Humans may forget details but the video recording of a particular play would provide the truth. In professional football, decision makers would always consult the video to confirm or dispute an assessment. If someone said, "This player has great game speed," or "That player gets stronger as the game goes on," then you could be sure that some grunt on the team staff would pull up film from that player's history and determine whether the assessment was accurate.

If I wanted to become a head coach, I would have to hone my ability to diagnose why a play wasn't successful and create ideas for how I could improve performance. The weekly grind of an NFL season meant that interventions must be made quickly. There wasn't any time for shareholder votes and strategic plans that would take years to implement. Every Sunday, grades were handed out and a player's, team's, or coach's stock would go either up or down. There wasn't much room for stagnation. If your value was flatlining, you were probably on your way out.

## MAKING THE GRADE

With Red Bull, coffee, and the Chiefs/Texans game video at my disposal, I tackled the grading process.[15] First, I printed grading sheets from the previous season. Then, I printed five blank sheets for

15    My Red Bull consumption for the 2007 season was roughly five cans per day for five straight months. That equates to roughly 66 gallons. I am not proud of this statistic.

Sunday's game. There were special teams plays to grade. This was going to be a long night.

Five hours of sleep sounded really good at the time, and for a few seconds my mind told me to not worry about this game and to just wait for the second game to practice my grading. The lazy side of my psyche was tugging on my fatigue. It was almost convincing. After all, Herm was not going to ask me to give a recap in the coaches' meeting this next morning. No one would ask for my opinion. But, I told myself, my lack of responsibility didn't matter. In due time I would have a seat at the table, and I would be expected to speak with certainty and confidence on every aspect of my role. There was no class at any school in the country that could prepare me for that moment. I was responsible for creating my own curriculum. This was my graduate school of coaching and I had to follow the honor code. No one would turn me in to the dean if I didn't complete my homework. I had the dual responsibilities of curriculum architect and study partner. So, with a deep sigh and a swig of Red Bull, I dove in.

Looking back on the decision to grade that first game, I am convinced that rejecting my physical impulse to "pack it in" made all the difference in my career. I know that each of us—at least those of us who seek out new lands and opportunities—finds ourselves at a critical moment where the choice is simple: Keep working or pack it in. The appealing nature of the status quo is a tough adversary. The status quo is comfortable and cozy. The alternative is a land of predators and tough terrain. You must rely on your desire and drive to do something others believe you are incapable of doing. That's all you need. Do you have it?

# TALE OF THE TAPE

As soon as I pressed Play, I noticed an obvious problem. The Chiefs and Texans were playing at two different speeds. Coaches often talk about "game speed," the pace of a player once the actual game starts, and it differs from practice speed. Some guys look great in practice, but once they reach prime time their energy level dips to an unexpected low. Some players look average in practice but can flip a switch that enables them to outpace the competition once the official clock begins.

What struck me as I compared the game speed of the Chiefs and Texans was how sluggish we were as a team. Sure, there were bursts of speed from some of our guys, but for the most part, we looked gassed. On paper, we had similar rosters and our size and speed appeared to match up pretty well. But the tape didn't lie: We didn't have the energy to compete.

For the first three plays the grading process was fairly simple. Our approach had been to keep the plays simple, according to Herm's general coaching philosophy—the KISS method (Keep It Simple, Stupid). Believers in this camp devised simple schemes that players could learn easily and execute with speed and confidence.

■ ■ ■

Herm, a coaching brother to Tony Dungy, was firmly in the KISS camp. After both men's playing careers ended, Dungy launched his coaching career while Herm chose a path that would lead him to the general manager's seat. Finally, Dungy convinced Herm to leave a scouting position with the Chiefs and serve as an assistant head coach and defensive backs coach for the Tampa Bay Buccaneers.

Dungy was known in coaching circles as a stickler for simplicity.

He constantly pushed his assistant coaches to water down the schemes so players could play with reckless abandon. He was a classic KISS coach, and his very basic Tampa 2 defensive scheme would help convert the Buccaneers from a perennial NFL joke to a Super Bowl contender.

When Herm took his first head coaching position with the New York Jets, he was an atypical choice because he had never served as a coordinator. Herm bypassed the position coach → coordinator → head coach path that had been followed by legions of men before him.

That he had spent the majority of his coaching career on the ground level, coaching players on the field and in the film room, meant that Herm had a knack for understanding how much players could absorb. "You're slowing him down," was a constant refrain in our coaches' meetings. Translation: Your plays require him to think too much. Simplify the system.

As I watched the Chiefs/Texans game unfold on an oversize projection screen, it was obvious that something needed to change—and quickly. The players who were taking the majority of special teams snaps were out of sync. Play after play, the same players were recording missed assignments. They looked lost, and it seemed like the game was too fast for them. Herm's preaching of simplification had converted me from a person who admired complexity to an aspiring coach who understood the need for ease and understanding, and it seemed that our players just weren't making it happen.

I wrote down my impressions of each play. I isolated what I thought were the breakdowns. For each player on each play, I assigned a plus (+) or minus (–). Then, I looked at the player's performance for the entire game and assigned a letter grade. I made educated guesses on *why* each player was performing below or above our expectations. I recorded my notes on how each player could improve. To bring the process full circle, I prescribed a set of drills that I believed could help each player rectify his deficiencies. If something stumped me, I left a blank and inserted a red question mark beside the play number. This process was arduous, and to be honest, I didn't know if most of what I was writing made any sense, but I continued to write. I wrote, wrote, and wrote some more. I cracked another can of Red Bull and then wrote some more. I did a few jumping jacks, threw some cold water on my face, and wrote some more. When I paused to look up at the clock, I couldn't believe it was already 4 a.m. Coaches would be arriving in thirty minutes. I gathered my papers, turned off the projector, and left the room.

As I expected, Gunther Cunningham strolled into the office at 4:30 a.m. He looked at me and said, "That was quite a stunt you pulled this weekend. You're out of your damn mind."

"You're not the first person to tell me that," I responded. "Besides, I'd rather fly to Houston and see the ass-kicking up close than watch it at a bar in KC."

"Fair point," he said. "Well, let's see what happens this weekend in Chicago. Everybody's on edge because we got our asses handed to us yesterday. Hopefully you make the plane this weekend. If not, don't get pissed off. That's just the business. Keep doing what you're doing," Gun advised.

"I gotta go look at this tape. It's not going to be good," he said, and he walked into his office.

I wasn't sure if I would have enough money to buy another plane ticket, so I had started to assess the cost of making the drive to Chicago.

It was approximately 511 miles from Kansas City to the Windy City. I could make that distance in about seven hours if I drove nonstop. With Saturday meetings ending around 11 a.m., it would be a tight window, but I might just be able to make it in time for night meetings. Nothing could go wrong between my departure and arrival, and I could not miss the Chicago game. After crashing the Houston party, it would be critical for me to double-down if I wanted to keep my stock's value rising.

Knowing that I would need an infusion of income to make ends meet, I reached out to my sister, who worked for a community college in my hometown. My days were filled with activities that required face time. After fulfilling my grunt duties at Arrowhead, I had to travel across town to Bishop Miege High School to serve as a volunteer defensive backs and special teams coach. Herm called Tim Grunhard, Miege's head football coach (and a former NFL center), and asked him to give me a chance to "coach on the grass." Herm knew I needed real coaching experience, and Grunhard was kind enough to let me improve my coaching skills as a member of his staff.

By the time I finished up at Miege, I would travel back to Arrowhead around seven o'clock. The experience was great—I got the opportunity to reenact the drills that I watched the pro coaches use each day—but the reality was that it left absolutely no time for any outside activities, like getting a paying job.

I did not want to call my sister—especially that early in the morning—but I was desperate. She was an administrator at a community college in my hometown, and I hoped she could help me secure an online teaching gig. Although I could cover most of my fixed costs, I was barely getting by—and I certainly couldn't afford to pay for many more road trips. I needed an injection of cash and I knew my sister could help me. In looking back on this experience, I can see that reaching that most humble and vulnerable point allowed me to secure a lifeline that would float me for the next six months.

For many people—especially those with aspirations of switching careers or starting new businesses—asking for help is analogous to taking the nuclear option. A reluctance or just plain fear to reach out to people seems to be a very common and unifying element. The mere thought of humbling themselves is simply too traumatic for them and they miss a helpful ingredient for achieving success—humility.

"Sonya, I need a favor," I began.

"Of course you do," she replied teasingly. "What do you need?"

"Well, I was wondering if your college needs any part-time professors."

"Daron, you're in Kansas City," she reminded me.

"Yes, I know, but I was wondering if I could teach some online classes. I could swing that and do my day job at the same time. I just need a little cash flow. What do you think? Any chance you could put in a good word for me?"

There was a long pause on the other end of the line.

"This could be tricky, but I will check. What classes would you teach?"

"Well, I was thinking that I could teach any English, economics, or government classes—anything liberal-artsy," I said.

"Okay, let me check, but you're sure you can handle your business there and teach a course, too? You know you're going to have to respond to emails and grade papers."

"Yes, I can make it happen. I appreciate you looking out for me, Sonya. A little cash would be really helpful right now."

"Okay, I will let you know. You need some extra money?"

"No, I'm good," I lied. "Thanks for offering, though. Okay, I gotta go. Thanks again."

It wasn't long before I was signed up to teach two online courses—econ and government. It took two days for me to create a syllabus and then post the content for each class online. As soon as the class went live, students started to email questions to me about assignments and grading policy.

With the steady income from my online teaching, I could plan to pay for at least one away game each month. I'd plan on driving to Chicago and look for law school buddies to crash with in the city. I could save on food costs by packing a few peanut butter and jelly sandwiches for the road. But, I realized, I had gotten ahead of myself: We hadn't even finished grading the Texans game.

## COMPARING NOTES

Slowly but surely, the rest of the coaching staff and players began to trudge through the door. The typical postgame meeting schedule for players, which after a loss could be described as the "March of Death," went like this:

7:00 a.m.—Training Room Opens (Injured Players)

8:30 a.m.—Team Meeting

8:45 a.m.—Special Teams Meeting

9:30 a.m.—Offensive/Defensive Meeting

10:00 a.m.—Position Group Meeting

11:45 a.m.—Lunch

What is not reflected in this schedule are the coaches' meetings that transpired before the team even arrived at the training facility. No one felt good about the previous day's performance. As the players ate breakfast and waited for the team meeting to start, coaches would huddle, debating how they could improve and whether some players should be swapped out for new ones.

As soon as I caught a glimpse of Prief rounding the corner to his office, I could tell he was not a happy camper. With close to fifteen years of coaching experience under his belt, it had taken him just over two hours to grade the film. I could only imagine the expletives bubbling under his breath as he clicked through the tape. Although the pundits had placed most of the blame for the loss on the special teams and offensive units, from the inside it was clear that our loss was the result of a colossal team meltdown.

Prief deposited a copy of his grade sheets on my desk.

"Make copies for every player and the head coach. Don't let anybody else see these grades. I'm serious, Daron, don't let anybody see them," Prief emphasized in unequivocal terms.

As I walked into the copy room, I felt like I had state secrets in my possession. I didn't know what would happen to me if an "unauthorized individual" got his hands on the grade sheets, but Prief had done a good job of putting the fear of God into me. I was imagining being brought before a federal judge on charges of treason or, even worse, getting kicked off the team.

I placed the sheet on the copier plate, chose Tray 4, and waited. Silence. I looked at my watch, and then back at the printer. I had ten minutes to get the copies made before the meeting.

On my fourth attempt and with eight minutes to go, the machine still would not respond to any button that I pressed. I was beginning to worry. I weighed my options. If I unplugged the machine and waited for the reboot, it would cost me two minutes. If I sprinted to the other side of the floor to use another printer, it would cost me two minutes *and* jeopardize the stealth nature of my assignment. So I unplugged the machine.

As expected, it powered down with the volume of a 757 coming in for landing. I waited five seconds, said a quick prayer, and plugged the machine back in. Green and red lights flashed and the initial signs looked promising. As soon as I saw the Ready light, I pressed the combination of buttons that were necessary to create double-sided, stapled, legal-sized copies with the precision of a seasoned paralegal. I pressed Start and prayed. I had six minutes until I had to turn the bundle over to Prief. Beads of sweat started to form on my forehead. Not only do I loathe being late, I was also very nervous about missing a deadline on the day after we had taken a beating.

I could feel my heart beating at an uncontrollable tempo. My fingers started to tremble, and the pit in my stomach slowly started to migrate into my throat. I was evaluating a list of potential excuses to use if I showed up late with the copies.

"The copier broke."

"The general manager asked me to work on a project."

"The head coach asked me to work on a project."

"The copier broke."

None were sufficient. Prief wouldn't care that the copier had broken. Like everyone else in the building, he only cared about results.

Sensing my nerves were going into overload, I used a practice I had learned in a yoga class a few years before. In my mind, my finger slowly drew the sides of an imaginary square. For each side of the shape, I spent five seconds drawing one side and breathing in. For the next side, I would exhale, then inhale for the next side, and then one final exhale at the end. I wouldn't dare tell anyone what I was doing (I was still a little self-conscious at the time) but my invisible square exercise was my reliable method of calming my nerves. I didn't focus on the copy machine or feet scurrying by. I tried to tune out the ticktock of the aged clock on the wall. All I cared about was getting around that square with care and calm.

When I opened my eyes, the copier was winding down. Within a few seconds, the final "ding" signaled the copy job was done. I grabbed the collated grade sheets and bolted for the door. People passing in the hallway were a blur. I walked into the meeting room, handed the papers to Prief, and took my seat in the back of the room.

The seating arrangement of coaches' meetings resembled the White House Cabinet. The head coach sat at the head of the table, flanked by the offensive and defensive coordinators. Position coaches occupied the rest of the seats at the table, and the grunts—that'd be my cohort—sat in the back. Even though the other coaches teased me about getting stuck in the "cheap seats," I knew I had the best perch in the house. I appointed myself as secretary and recorded both the dialogue and my impressions of the proceedings.

Herm sat down and everyone else straightened up. He started with Prief, asking three simple questions: What did your unit do well? What did your unit not do well? What is your plan to get better? He expected accountability. As each coach reported on the previous day's performance, they repeated the same refrain: "We practiced this a million times." But no one could explain why we weren't executing the plays at a high rate.

# THE DEBRIEF

Herm took center stage before the players at 8:30 a.m. on the dot. This was the first time he would address the team since we had returned to Kansas City. My job was simply to close the doors as soon as he took the floor. Anyone who wasn't in that room by the time I closed the doors was either getting fined, fired, or both. Team meetings were sacred.

Players sat at attention. Everyone knew that Herm's perspective had sharpened since watching the tape. Houston played with more energy and execution. What was more troubling: It looked as if we didn't have the chutzpah to play a solid fourth quarter. That oft-heard cliché—games are won in the fourth quarter—is a truism. Good teams mustered the energy to finish opponents in the fourth quarter. Great teams didn't have to. We were neither.

Herm gave us one directive: Do Your Job. It sounded simple, but the tape showed players trying to compensate for others' shortcomings instead of executing their own assignments. This "compensation cycle" could easily spiral out of control, and it had in the Texans game. The result was a game in which no one had done their job. If we were to have any chance of beating the Bears, we would have to take an honest inventory of our mistakes, draw up a plan to correct them, and start building a new game plan.

Heads nodded. The room was in agreement. We broke the meeting and headed to our respective special teams meetings and then on to position meetings. Herm's team meeting represented a macro look at how the team performed. From there we drilled a level deeper, to the unit side of the ball game. From there, we went to the micro level, the position meeting. In this meeting, the position coaches would drill down to the essentials. As I sat in the defensive backs' meeting, Coach David Gibbs coached each defensive back on every single play on their alignment, assignment, and technique.

- Alignment: Be where you're supposed to be.
- Assignment: Do what you're supposed to do.
- Technique: Do it how you're supposed to do it.

This rubric can be applied to any performance-driven profession. Whether a chef or consultant, a productive individual must be "present." Being present is different from simply being in a location. Being present requires a person to bring his entire being to a location. It requires him to shed a preoccupation with otherness. The flashing light of a phone, wondering about what genre of food will be served for dinner—these are the types of distractions that pull a person from being present and settle that person into the land of simply being there.

Next, people must understand what their assignment is. Understanding the assignment is difficult. If you were to randomly walk into the offices of one hundred professionals and ask them what their assignment was, you would probably get a mixed garble of nonsense that was tangentially related to their job. The assignment is a micro-level understanding of what has to be done. Most people go through the motions and shuffle paper from one office to the next, but being able to articulate the assignment at hand is critical for success.

Simply put, the great ones do it the way that it is supposed to be done. If the route calls for a ninety-degree cut at ten yards, then the great ones make the ninety-degree cut at ten yards. Average players make the cut at eight yards and the above-average get to nine. The impressive trait of the great ones is their appreciation of details. To watch a player like Tony Gonzalez, a man considered to be one of the great tight ends in the game, was to study a man dedicated to the minutiae of his job. The playbook was the Bible and he followed it to the letter. And by fulfilling his alignment, assignment, and technique, he was able to reach the fourth level—creativity. The logic-defying catches that flashed across the screen on ESPN were by-products of knowing the assignment, alignment, and technique required to make each play succeed and, after checking off those boxes, having the courage to create the improbable.

But for now, we weren't producing any highlight material. We needed to get back to basics.

## PIVOT POINTS

1  Understand the difference between the preseason and regular season. Play your game accordingly.

2  Grade yourself honestly. Regularly examine whether you understand the concepts that are the critical building blocks of your profession.

3  Sit in the back and soak up the action.

4  Do your job, and do it the way it is supposed to be done.

# CHAPTER 6

# HUG A TREE

After the players left the building on Monday, preparation for the Chicago game began in earnest. We had a twenty-four-hour rule—win or lose, we would focus on the previous opponent for no more than twenty-four hours after the game. Then we would move on to the next opponent. So on Monday evening, I sat down with a fresh cup of coffee and began to draft my scouting report on the Bears.

In practices, the team would spend the next four days concentrating on the basics: tackling and catching. While I tried to concentrate on doing my job, it was getting harder and harder to suppress the worry that I wouldn't make the plane. Nate, my best source of information on the inside, was tight-lipped. I strolled into his office on Wednesday morning.

"So, Nate, you think I'm going to make the plane?"

He stared at me. "Hey, man, I got all sorts of stuff going on right now. I got no clue. Let's see what Carl decides."

"When do you think we will know?" I asked.

"I would say late tomorrow, early Friday. By then, you should have an answer."

I went straight to my laptop to send an email to my law school buddy, Chris Richardson, who was practicing in Chicago. I was fairly certain he would let me crash if I needed a place to stay, but I didn't want to ask too late.

Chris—

*I hope all is going well, big dog. All is good here, other than the fact that we're 0–1. How's firm life?*

*Hey man, I may need a favor from you . . . looks like I may need a place to crash this weekend in Chicago. Any chance I can use your couch for Saturday night? I don't snore.—DKR*

It didn't take long for him to respond.

D—

*What's up man? All is well, bro . . . well it's about as good as it can be . . . just slaving away at the firm.*

*Anyway, you don't have to ask. The couch is yours. Let me know if you need it.—C Rich*

With that, I began to map the best route to Chicago. Thursday came and went without incident and then finally Nate walked nonchalantly into the press box.

"Hey, man, can you make copies of this for me?"

"Sure," I said. I was so engrossed in finishing up my checklist for the Chicago trip that I didn't notice what he dropped on my desk.

**"Game 2: KC @ Chi. September 16, 2007. Plane Manifest."**

My heart stopped. I ran my finger down the list, from first class all the way through coach. There I was, "Daron Roberts," in seat 44E.

I didn't want to believe it. I had been tricked before. I went into Nate's office. "Did you see this?" I asked Nate.

"Of course I saw it. Congrats again," he chuckled.

"What are the odds that I don't get bumped this time?

"You're in, D. Word got out about that stunt that you pulled in Houston. You're in," Nate said.

I made his copies, zipped through the building, and got them back to the press box as fast as I could.

I called my parents and whispered, "I made the plane for the Chicago game. It's real this time."

# THE SKIES OPEN, AGAIN

It was official: I would be traveling with the team during the regular season. My gamble during the first game had paid off. The rumor was that a couple of people had mentioned to the general manager that I traveled to Houston on my own dime. Although Herm never said anything to me about getting bumped from the plane for the opening game, I felt certain that he had gone to bat for me. He was the only person who had the clout to get me on the manifest. That he never mentioned my change in status didn't surprise me. Herm's style of leadership centered on action over credit. If you want to help someone, just do it. Period. And don't expect a confetti party in reward for good work. Just keep working. So that's what I did.

Now that I didn't have to plan a five-hundred-mile drive to Chicago, I could turn my full attention to improving as a coach.[16] I was getting a first-rate education working with special teams and defense, but knowledge alone was not going to accelerate my climb up the coaching ladder. I needed to expand my network past the confines of Arrowhead Stadium. That meant I needed to reach out to more coaches and engender relationships.

At the season opener, I noticed how many coaches and players from the two teams spent time joshing each other, hugging, and catching up before kickoff. It was a part of the NFL culture that many fans never got a chance to see. Broadcast coverage focused on the players fighting it out until the bitter end. But in reality, many coaches and players on both teams knew each other from youth football leagues, college rivalries, and former NFL rosters. Relationships matured and developed as players and coaches moved between leagues and teams. As I watched this weekly pregame reunion ritual unfold, I felt a little jealous. As a rookie grunt without any college playing experience, I didn't have these same friendships.

I had experienced this in my pre-NFL days at Harvard, as well. Harvard students were fixated on meeting as many other Harvard people as they could. The people at the Kennedy School were trying

---

16    To be honest, I had been looking forward to a solo road trip in my gray Tahoe with 2Pac, the Eagles, and Eric Clapton rotating through the CD player.

to meet the people at Harvard Law School, who were trying to meet the people at Harvard Business School. Students would shake hands, exchange pleasantries, and try to predict whether the person on the other side of the conversation would do something worthwhile enough in their professional life to warrant continuing the dialogue. After a couple of follow-up emails, both parties would walk away feeling as if they had fulfilled their networking duties.

Networking is absolutely critical to professional success, but I have noticed that the most successful professionals are those who are vigilant in tending their nets. They don't just meet people for the sake of meeting people. They meet people, and if a connection sparks, they reach back with care and consideration. They use personal stationery to solidify an impact. They send emails that add value. They include updates related to the person's industry or comment on a specific achievement. For example, here's a note I wrote to a coach:

*Coach Walton,*

*Hope all is well. I watched your matchup against Buffalo last night. You guys had an incredible blitz plan for third downs. Good luck the rest of the season.*

*DKR*

Maintaining a connection is as simple as that.

So, on the Friday night before the Bears game, I revisited the notes that I had taken from all of the coaching books I read before training camp. Over and over, a theme rose to the surface: the coaching tree. Vince Lombardi, Bill Walsh, Chuck Noll—every great coach was a descendant of a coaching lineage. This extended family of coaches provided a dependable network of men to offer advice and help with advancing to the next level.

Herm's rise as a head coach was a prime example. The rumor around the League was that when Woody Johnson, owner of the New York Jets, called Tony Dungy about his head coaching vacancy, Dungy had a recommendation for him: Hire Herm Edwards. Tapping Herm for head coach ran counter to NFL conventional wisdom. Not only had he never served as a head coach, he had never served as a coordinator. But Dungy saw in Edwards a potential to lead an organization at an early age. Johnson took the recommendation and Herm was named as the Jets head coach in 2001.

Herm's football lineage read like the first chapter of Matthew:

Sid Gillman begat Chuck Noll.

Chuck Noll begat Tony Dungy.

Tony Dungy begat Herm Edwards.

The NFL is a forest of coaching trees. An originator creates a philosophy and vision, then leafs out the branches of his tree with coaches who can carry out his mission. Assistant coaches eventually get head coaching jobs and do the same thing. And guess where those head coaches pluck their talent from? That's right—the branches of their coaching tree. Whether you're an aspiring investment banker or a budding interior designer, you must nurture and cultivate your tree. A tree offers many more benefits than a mentor. It offers many branches of knowledge and support.

The first step in cultivating your tree is to articulate your vision and commence a relentless search for the people in your industry who hold a similar philosophy. Then the ~~stalking~~ courting period begins. Find the closest branch and make every human effort to cultivate a relationship. Collect every article you can find that provides insights on that person's journey. Send emails and letters. Buy every book the target has written. Find where this person will be speaking and attend.

When I was trying to break into the NFL, I knew that I wanted to join the Tony Dungy coaching tree, so I gathered everything that I could find on him—old newspaper articles, magazine stories, and grainy YouTube videos. Now that I was in the NFL ecosystem, it was time to take my investigative approach into the regular season. I needed to connect with the coaches and execs on the other side of the field before I ever reached the stadium.

After our first game, I decided to memorize the names and backgrounds of the opposing coaches and scouts that we would encounter each Sunday. I ~~stole~~ borrowed a pack of index cards from the office supply room. For an opposing team, I wrote the name of each coach on a card, flipped the card, and wrote three facts. For example, for Lovie Smith, I wrote the following: (1) Bears head coach, (2) linebackers coach for Tony Dungy at Tampa, (3) from Big Sandy, Texas. I remembered that last nugget from my letter-writing campaign and it was of particular interest to me. Big Sandy is less than fifty miles from my hometown of Mount Pleasant.

I made it my goal to meet at least three coaches before each game. I practiced my intro. I didn't want it to sound canned, but I also wanted to memorize the script so I wouldn't waste time trying to think of something witty. I had to keep it simple, stupid. Delivery was key. I looked in the mirror and practiced with the vigor of an adolescent boy getting ready for his first dance.

A large part of the reason why I was practicing so intently

was because I had caved under pressure in the offseason. Unsure of myself, I was reluctant to reach out to people from other teams. We had played the Bears in the preseason, and I was determined to introduce myself to Lovie. But it didn't happen because I cowered. I watched him for thirty minutes during our pregame warm-up, but failed to seize the opportunity to introduce myself. After that game, I decided that I would not let that happen again.

Another tactic in my research was to monitor key NFL websites for news updates on the upcoming opponent. This was not a part of my job, but in an effort to find ways to add value, I scoured the Internet for any information I could gather on injuries, team politics, or indications of a coach tipping his hand on his team's approach for an upcoming game. An NFL game is like a classic poker match and, under the right conditions, a player or coach could make a seemingly benign statement that would offer a critical clue for the upcoming match.

The industry standard for the inside scoop was (and still is) Profootballtalk.com.[17] I checked the site at least twenty times a day. I also added Yahoo Sports and ESPN to the rotation. As Coach Gibbs would say, "You gotta be an information provider in this business. People need an edge and if you can give it to them, you will go far." At times I didn't know what I was looking for, but anything that related to our upcoming opponent seemed like good material.

I have found this practice to be extremely beneficial in every

---

17    The website was started by a guy who charted a path similar to mine. Mike Florio graduated from West Virginia University's law school, practiced for nearly two decades, and then decided to create a rumor site for the NFL. He had moonlighted for ESPN.com for six months before striking out on his own. If you wanted to know who was getting fired or hired and what trades were looming on the horizon, PFT was the place to go.

sector that I've worked in. Whether working as an aide in the US Senate or as an executive in higher education, staying in touch with the major developments in one's profession is critical to being able to see around the corner. More important, it empowers you to craft solutions with more time to deliberate. This distinction is the difference between being a reactionary or a proactive force.

## ELIMINATE THE CLUTTER (ETC)

As soon as we completed our last walk-through on Saturday, I headed for the showers. I wanted to make sure that I gave myself enough time to get dressed and review my checklist before boarding the plane. After being first out of the shower, I threw on my charcoal gray suit, white button-down, and solid red tie. Chiefs colors. "Keep it simple, stupid" was also my motto for dressing the part.

One could say that my style was the antithesis of what *GQ* magazine would recommend for men in 2007. Case in point: When I first started working with the team, there were all sorts of varieties of shoes, shorts, shirts, socks, and caps. Once I found the combination of clothing that I liked, I went to the equipment room and struck a deal—I would not need to be issued any additional clothing options if I could get multiple sets of gray shorts and white shirts. The equipment manager on duty just stared at me blankly. He was accustomed to people asking for all sorts of NFL goodies, but I was asking for less. Within a day, I had six pairs of gray shorts and six white shirts. I was set until the winter, and I never had to figure out what shirt corresponded with what shorts.

My mission was to simplify my life as much as possible. I wanted to unclutter my mind of the inconsequential so I could focus on high-level goals. To me, researching the backgrounds of every coach and scout on the Bears team was a high-level pursuit. Putting together a special teams scouting report on the Bears was a high-level pursuit. Deliberating for more than twenty seconds on which suit/tie/shirt combination to wear for an away game was a *low-value activity*. To simplify it even further, I enlisted help from my mom. As an expert shopper, she was a pro at finding great deals. As a former law clerk, I had a ton of suits, but my shirt collection was lacking. I gave her my shirt measurements and asked if she could be on the lookout for white button-down shirts, preferably the non-iron variety, to help me save time and money on pressing my shirts. In less than two weeks, I received a shipment from L.L. Bean. Inside were ten white shirts.[18] I was set for the season. Heck, I was set for the decade.

As I was tying my tie, Coach Krumrie, our defensive line coach, walked by. He stopped.

Krummie scanned me from neck to shoes. "Looks like somebody's getting ready for the prom!" he yelped.

Some of the other guys started laughing. A jolt of self-consciousness shot through my body. I paused and evaluated. If I volleyed back I'd never hear the end of it. I smiled, finished the knot in my tie, grabbed my bag, and walked out of the locker room. As I walked out, I could hear the jeers, "Harvard Boy headed for his debate tournament." I didn't let it bother me at all. My end goal wasn't to become an assistant coach; I wanted to become a head coach. Now was the time for me to dress the part.

18    Having a single color of shirt made the weekly decision-making process that much easier. Wasting time in one's closet is no way to live.

In my mind, I was executing each and every step that I would eventually take as a head coach. I thought about where I would sit on the plane. Like Herm, I would sit at the very back, in coach with the majority of the team. I thought about the order of meetings for the Saturday night prep session. I thought about what the meal options would be for Saturday night's dinner and Sunday's breakfast. For each of these points, I scribbled my impressions of what I liked, what I didn't like, and what I would change. These details may seem like small matters, but I didn't view them that way. I saw them as the elements that would form my identity and philosophy.

As we made our way to Kansas City Airport, I had a brief panic attack that I'd get turned away trying to board the plane. I could just imagine showing my ID at the gate, only to be told that I would have to turn around because my name was not on the manifest.

When we reached the airport, I nervously exited the bus with my roller and satchel and followed the line for security. I reached the front of the line, pulled out my ID, and waited. The security guard looked down at his list. He flipped a page. He flipped another page. My worst nightmare was unfolding and it was pure torture.

"Oh, here we go, 'Roberts.' I got you right here."

I boarded the plane, took my seat, and breathed a huge sigh of relief.

# THE WINDY CITY

As soon as we boarded the buses to take us from the airport to the hotel, I started reviewing my scouting reports. Chiefs versus Bears was a pivotal game. The feeling was that our performance in this game would be a good indication of what type of season we would have. I wasn't prepared to hang the outlook for our entire season on our second game, but I knew we needed to win this one and I could sense the collective tension in the air. A motorcade escorted the buses through what would normally have been congested Chicago streets, and within twenty minutes we arrived at our destination.

We had to wade through the usual suspects, visitors gathered in front of the hotel to greet us. At the very front were the ever-present memorabilia collectors. Behind them, family members of the players were waiting. Mothers and brothers adorned with jerseys were walking billboards. Girlfriends and college buddies made up the fringe.

The memorabilia collectors—middle-aged guys, mostly—carried stacks of player head shots. They carried bags of helmets and jerseys. Like me, they had Sharpies in every pocket. As soon as they spotted a player, they'd reach inside their bag, pull out his head shot, jersey, and helmet, and chase him down.

This scene raised a question for me: How did the autograph seekers find out which hotel we were staying at? Going back to the preseason, I had been to four different cities—Cleveland, St. Louis, Houston, and Chicago—and in every city the scene was exactly the same. I couldn't help but wonder if there wasn't a lucrative black market for information like this. Who was the mole and how much was he or she getting paid? Was the leak in our organization? The hotel? The travel agency?

As soon as I walked into the lobby, I spotted a row of tables with the usual alphabetical designations: A–F, G–L, et cetera. I picked up the Roberts, D. envelope with my key cards and headed to my room to set up everything I would need for Sunday morning. I laid out my outfit for the following day and sat down to review the itinerary for the rest of the evening:

6:00 p.m.—Special Teams Meeting

7:00 p.m.—Offense/Defense Meeting

8:00 p.m.—Team Meeting

8:30 p.m.—Dinner

10:00 p.m.—Bed Check

Just as I began to write a few notes, my cell rang. It was Chris. "Hey, man, you make it into Chicago alright?" he asked.

"Yes, indeed. No glitches. I was nervous they might kick me off of the plane, but everything was smooth," I responded.

"So what's up for tonight? You gonna have time to get together?" he asked.

"That's gonna be tough. We got a jam-packed schedule and I'm on the first bus tomorrow morning. If I kick it with you, I may end up hungover and late. I better play it safe."

We both laughed. We had spent several long nights in Harvard Square, drinking away our sorrows and dreaming of a day when we would be free from the bondage of law school.

"Well alright, man. Good luck tomorrow. Get the job done."

"Appreciate that, buddy. Thanks again."

The time was 4:15 p.m., and I was tired. I flipped on the TV to check in on the college games. I could feel my eyelids growing heavier and heavier. I snapped back to consciousness. My heart skipped a beat. Now, the worst-case scenarios started to flow through my mind. What if I fell asleep and missed the evening meetings? What if

I overslept and missed the Sunday morning buses? I was paranoid. I jumped up, ran to the windows, and drew the curtains back. I needed as much light as possible to keep me from dozing off. Then, I called the front desk.

"Good evening, Mr. Roberts, how may I help you?"

"Yes, I need to schedule six wake-up calls."

"Excuse me, sir, did you say *six* wake-up calls?"

"Yes, may I get wake-up calls at 5:15 p.m., 5:20 p.m., and 5:25 p.m. this evening and then 7:15 a.m. and 7:20 a.m. and 7:25 a.m. tomorrow morning?"

Silence.

"Mr. Roberts, you do realize that our system keeps calling if you do not answer our initial wake-up call? It's a built-in way to make sure that you wake up if you are in a deep sleep."

"Yes, I realize this. May I just get the ~~damn~~ six wake-up calls, please?"

"Of course, Mr. Roberts. I will schedule your calls now. Is there anything else that I can assist you with this evening?"

"No, ma'am, that will be it. I appreciate your patience."

"Certainly, Mr. Roberts, enjoy your stay."

Overkill? Maybe. But this was a high-stakes game and I would not take even one risk. Since I had been averaging four hours of sleep a night, I knew that I was a prime candidate for oversleeping.

Scheduling the wake-up calls did not ease my paranoia.

I set six alarms on my cell phone: 5:16 p.m., 5:21 p.m., 5:26 p.m., 7:16 a.m., 7:21 a.m., and 7:26 a.m. Then, I opened my laptop and repeated the exercise. There was no way I would miss a single meeting or the team bus the following morning.

I couldn't sit still, so I decided to go into the bathroom, stand in front of the mirror, and play head coach for a while. What would Herm say to his team at the evening meeting? He stressed the same simple mantra during the whole week. "Know your role. Do your job. Play fast." As I examined the refrain, I noticed the power of the single-syllable word. Short, punchy words leave an impression. If you woke me up at three in the morning, I could recite the three commands with ease. Then I realized there is also power in three. There was a rhythm and a symmetry in the construction of three key points that made the message easy to remember. I took note of the power of being able to state my worldview in a short, three-sentence pitch as part of my philosophy for running a team.

It wasn't quite time to head to the meetings, but I was so antsy that I decided to head downstairs and hang around the meeting room to see what was happening. When I arrived on the conference room floor, I passed security and walked by the defensive meeting room. Gun, ever vigilant, was watching a clip of the Chicago Bears offense. Gibby saw me and yelled, "Hey, what are you doing?"

"Nothing," I said. "Just hanging out before the meetings start."

"Follow me."

I walked with Gibby down the hallway into a dimly lit room with chairs arranged in a circle. Gibby pulled up a chair on the outside of the ring.

"Sit here and listen. Take this and give it back to me when the meeting is over."

As I flipped through the packet he had given me, I could see that it was a quiz for the defensive backs. The plays that could hurt us the most were diagrammed with questions underneath.

The players filed in and took seats around the circle. No one spoke. Everyone looked at their packets and waited for Gibby to start the meeting.

"Okay, let's get to it. Benny, you're up first, what's the answer to the first question?"

Benny Sapp, an undrafted college free agent from Northern Iowa, was in his fourth season with the team. He was primarily a nickel player—he specialized in playing on third-down plays, when the probability of a pass play was the highest. At five feet nine and 185 pounds, he was small, but smart and quick-footed.

He rattled off the answer. This routine continued as Gibby put players on the spot, one by one, to ensure all questions were answered. What struck me was the coach's response when a player stated the wrong answer. His first question would be, "Okay, what was your thought process?" As the player walked through his decision path, Gibby would interject. "Okay, stop there. Let's think about this." He was applying the Socratic method to football coaching. My law school professors would have been impressed.

Gibby's process unfolded over and over and by the end of the meeting, all questions were answered and the entire unit felt as if they were on the same page. It had been obvious in the previous week's practices that the defensive secondary unit was especially in need of building teamwork. The secondary represents the last line of defense—nothing separates the offense from the end zone but that defensive unit. Gibby had to ensure that the group was on the same page for us to have a chance to win.

After the meeting ended, Gibby huddled up the players and let the veterans say some parting words. As the guys started to leave the room, I turned to Gibby and said, "That was good stuff."

"My job is to make sure they are mentally prepared." Gibby shrugged. "All I can do is put them in the position to make a play. We watch tape, we hit the field, we talk through progressions, and I end the week with a test. Their job is to make the play. Remember that, a coach's job is to put his players in a position to make a play."

As we headed to the defensive meeting, the mood changed. Gun called everyone to attention.

"Okay, let's stop jacking around. It's time to get down to business. Remember, this is not college. This is your job. Herm says the same thing every week—'Know your role. Do your job. Play fast.' That's exactly what we have to do tomorrow if we want to win."

Gun's preferred method of teaching was a variation on the Socratic method. He pressed Play on the remote and pulled a cutup of thirty plays.[19] "Alright," he yelled, "linebackers, make the call." The linebackers would chime in with the call—"Closed left" or "Closed right." Just as on the field, the call would initiate a ripple effect. The defensive line would immediately know which way to line up and the secondary would make the necessary adjustments on the back end. It all hinged on the linebacker making the right call. If that call was wrong, it would create a chain reaction of faulty calls, and the probability of giving up a big play would skyrocket. This player interdependency is the foundation of a good football team. The real-time communication that needed to occur in order to execute the most simplistic of plays was akin to the NASA Mission Control Center's back-and-forth with a space shuttle.

19   A cutup is a selection of individual football plays arranged into a continuous reel.

While most observers focused on the readily quantifiable bag of stats that travel with a player from team to team, they overlooked the importance of a well-functioning communication system.

As Gun's narration formed a soundtrack to the flashes on the projector screen, I took a moment to think about the importance of what was happening. There were thousands of little league, high school, and college football coaches who dreamed of getting just a glimpse of what I was taking part in. And to think that a year before, I was sitting in my constitutional law class having exactly that daydream.

I looked around and took note of the assorted flavors of body language on display. Veterans leaned back in their chairs, hands folded on their chests, watching the reel unfold. Players entering the last year of their contracts were listening intently, leaning in to the lesson. And then there were the bubble players—players signed to one-year contracts, draft picks, and college free agents. The smart ones had notebooks out, writing feverishly as they looked from screen to page. Their jobs were at stake. Mortgages were on the line. Expensive lifestyles were in the balance. One high-profile misstep could result in the dreaded "Ray wants to see you" message. A summons from Ray Farmer, director of pro personnel, could be your last meeting in Arrowhead. He delivered the decision to keep, trade, or cut a player.

Just a week earlier, our rookie kicker, Justin Medlock, was cut less than twenty-four hours after he missed a thirty-yard field goal attempt. With an understanding of the task ahead, we headed to Herm's meeting.

In pure Herm fashion, he kept his remarks brief and to the point. Tomorrow would be a chance to show the rest of the League what kind of team we had. We had not performed to the level that we were capable of in Houston. At the end, Herm reminded everyone to "trust your brother to do his job. And, make sure you do yours."

We migrated from the team meeting room to the dining room. I prepared a meal to go and went back to my room. This wasn't any time for small talk. I needed to prepare for my own plays on the field.

I had a list of three people to approach: Lovie Smith, Darryl Drake, and Gill Byrd. Darryl Drake was the Bears' wide receivers coach and had spent a few years coaching at the University of Texas during my time as an undergrad. That was my hook. Gill Byrd was the Bears' assistant defensive backs coach. While his background didn't provide any convenient hooks for me to use, he had achieved the coaching position that I wanted to get in a couple of years. And Lovie Smith? Well, I needed no other reason than that he was the Bears' head coach.

I awoke at 7:00 a.m. and went for a run. With a 3:15 p.m. kickoff, I had some time and some nervous energy to burn before boarding the bus. After a long run, I grabbed breakfast, got dressed, and waited in the lobby. I jumped on the first bus that pulled up and we headed to Soldier Field.

I used the time to review my index cards. Upon entering the stadium, I walked into the locker room and set my things up in a corner, courtesy of my 3M plastic hook, and changed into my game-day clothes. As the locker room became more congested, I gathered my notepad, Sharpies, pens, and stopwatches (I brought two this time) and headed for the field.

The field was dotted with the usual three-ring circus of players going through their pregame machinations. Each team was also working out a few injured players to see if they could move well enough to make it onto the active roster for the day. Before kickoff, teams had to designate the forty-six players who would be "active" for the day. Each week, some of those decisions would take place the day of the game, as teams waited to see how a player's body felt after Saturday night's sleep.

As I looked over the field, I didn't see any of my primary targets, so I decided to take a walk around the sidelines. I only had a few minutes until I had to chart kicks. As I walked, I noticed Gill approaching the field. He was on the opposite sideline and it looked like he was talking to a groundskeeper. I slowly approached him and stuck out my hand. "Gill, Daron Roberts, how's it going?"

"Good, man!" he replied. I could tell that he was wondering who in the hell I was. I mustered the courage to keep going. "I'm working with special teams and defense. Started up in training camp. Got any advice on how to survive?"

"Ha! Man, that's a good one. If you find the answer, let me know. In all seriousness, keep your head down and keep good notes. Also, soak up that special teams stuff. If you can coach special teams, then you can get a job in college. Those guys gotta coach a position *and* coach a unit on special teams."

"You ever thought about coaching in college?" I asked, trying to keep the conversation going.

"Sure, but I got a good thing going here. Just remember though, never close any doors."

And with that, he walked away. I took out my notebook and jotted down his advice.

Our specialists hit the field and were ready to go. It was time to chart kicks. We had picked up a new kicker, Dave Rayner, earlier in the week. I was looking forward to observing his pregame routine.

But first, our long snapper had to remind me that he remembered my oversight from the previous week.

"I see you brought your stopwatch this time," J. P. whispered.

I just smiled and clicked the timer button.

This charting session was tougher than others—I couldn't help but keep an eye out for Drake and Coach Smith. As the kickers finished up, I finally saw Drake warming up some of his receivers. I jogged over, offered him a handshake, and said, "Daron Roberts. I'm working with special teams and defense. I was a student at Texas while you were coaching there. How's it going?"

"Man, it's all good. I miss Austin weather sometimes."

I could tell it was a bad time. His eyes were scanning the field.

"Hey, man, good luck today. I'll catch up with you," I said.

And with that I made my way for Coach Smith. He was chatting with Herm at midfield and so I paced the sideline until they finished up, then I made my move.

"Coach Smith. I'm working with special teams and defense. Started up in training camp. Herm kept me for the season. I'm originally from Mount Pleasant."

I paused. Lovie just looked at me.

"Mount Pleasant . . . that's not far from where I grew up," he said. This was the cue I was waiting for.

"Right, about forty miles. It's a good part of the country."

"Yes indeed," he responded.

I could tell the clock was ticking.

"Well, I just wanted to introduce myself. I hope to get a chance to see you at the Combine."

"Sounds good," he said. "Look for me."

And with that I had gone three for three. Although my conversation with Drake hadn't been that great, I had still met my goal. I would write follow-up notes as soon as I got back to Kansas City.

The easiest part of networking is always the introduction—the initial conversation. While most people obsess over this element, they don't spend enough time concentrating on the "reach-back" phase, which is the tactic that separates you from the countless encounters that a person has. It is the toughest phase because it requires diligence. At its core, it requires a sacrifice of ego and a commitment to play the long game. For most people, it's much easier to simply meet people for drinks at an after-work event and send a short email the next day. This is the way of the masses. But to make a meaningful reach-back and connect on a different level, the personal touch of a handwritten note is so rare that the mere sight of an envelope in the mail startles people. Short emails (actually emails in general) tend to blend into the email ecosystem without making a deep impression. But handwritten notes force the recipient to take deliberate steps—like find a letter opener and physically free the letter from the envelope. The ease of hitting "send" has forced the value of emails to plunge to near-record lows. Meanwhile, the value of a handwritten note continues to soar as the coalition of willing writers gets smaller.

## A SECOND LOSS

After a scoreless first quarter, it looked as if this game was going to be a battle until the final minutes. I shuffled papers between the printer and Prief. The team seemed upbeat. Herm paced the sideline, clapping his approval at the effort, and our guys played with the intensity of a team trying to reach .500.

And then we were into the second quarter.

Devin Hester, the greatest fear of every special teams coordinator, did exactly what he was feared for: He returned a seventy-three-yard punt for a touchdown. Coupled with an improbable touchdown thrown to an offensive tackle, the score rose to 14–0 in short order. As I transported the printout of Hester's touchdown to Priefer, I braced myself for the paper cuts that I would have after he snatched the sheets from my hands. Surprisingly, he took the printouts politely and looked at the image.

"Yep, just what I thought," he said, and he stomped off toward a special teams player in his sights.

The rest of the day followed suit. Our offensive units could only muster one touchdown, and as the final seconds ticked off the clock, we stared at a 0–2 record. The score stood at 20–10, Bears. As I walked off of Soldier Field, I knew the next week would feature some fireworks. Things were about to get interesting.

■ ■ ■

Looking back on that moment in my personal development, I can be critical of the things that I didn't do well. I should have engaged other Chiefs coaches on a deeper level, and I should have asked more questions about the process that was unfolding before my eyes. We were about to enter a critical phase in the life cycle of the organization, and a "translator" would have helped me to understand some of the decisions I was about to see. On the other hand, I know my approach to expanding my non-Chiefs coaching circle was extremely beneficial. Many of the relationships that I cultivated that year were instrumental in my growth as a coach.

The critical lesson is that cultivating professional relationships must be an intentional process. It requires performing due diligence with a tax attorney's attention to detail. I was determined to gather as much information as possible about the people I would meet. I committed important biographical details to memory. I practiced my introduction. Then, I considered the different paths that our conversation could take. This approach was similar to the framework that I learned from Arthur Miller, my civil procedure professor. Every branch of the decision tree must be examined ("Well, what if he says this? What if he says that?"). Exploring this thought process allows you to have an edge in your first encounter. Some people call this level of research "stalking." I prefer to call it "performing due diligence."

Any edge—whether natural or engineered—is an edge.

## PIVOT POINTS

1   Research your "family tree" and keep an updated version of its members.

2   Be an information provider. Know the major news sources in your profession and stay abreast of any developments.

3   ETC—Eliminate the clutter. Spend less time on low-value activities.

4   Dress how you want to be addressed.

5   Put yourself in a position to make a play. Then make your play.

6   Research. Reach out. Reach back.

# CHAPTER 7

# TRUST THE SYSTEM

The return flight to Kansas City was quiet.

The air tasted like disappointment mixed with a splash of panic. *Are we this bad?* That was the question on everyone's mind. I couldn't help but think back to how we looked in the preseason. There were flashes of success during those first four exhibition games that created some optimism for the upcoming season. But the reality was that the regular season was a different world. The pace of the game had ramped up to a speed that we could not meet. Something had to change. Or even worse, *someone* had to change.

The previous week's loss claimed the contract of our fifth-round kicker. Now, the players looked around at each other. Who would be the next to go? With the exception of two sacred cows, ninety-eight percent of the roster was expendable.[20] Although most of the pundits had blamed the offense and special teams for our woes, no one felt good about the general direction of the entire team. From top to bottom, soul-searching, hand-wringing, and old-fashioned worry were taking place in the building.

As soon as we made it back to Arrowhead, I started a pot of coffee. It would be another long night of self-inflicted grading. But I had a few critical tasks of my own that I needed to cross off my list. First, I wrote short notes to my three targets. I had a general rule with reach-back notes—write them within twenty-four hours of the encounter. I didn't have any reliable stats to support my theory, but I guessed that the likelihood of a person writing a follow-up note declined by at least forty-five percent if not written within the twenty-four-hour period after the encounter. And with email being the preferred method of communication, I was sure that hardly anyone was writing letters anyway. Although I really wanted to take a quick nap before getting back to the grind, I fought the urge and sat down to write. The note to Lovie read like this:

> *Dear Coach Smith,*
>
> *Thank you for taking the time to talk with me on Sunday.❶ It was a pleasure to meet you. Since your entry into the League, I have admired at your ability to lead men by providing an example of integrity.❷ Good luck the rest of the season.*
>
> *Sincerely,*
>
> *Daron K. Roberts*
>
>
> *PS. You're right, East Texas is a good part of the country.❸*

20    These two cows were: Jared Allen (defensive end) and Tony Gonzalez (tight end). The former was our best defensive player. The latter was one of the best tight ends in the history of football. To see what eventually happened to Allen, see Chapter 10.

In each note I featured three points: 1) gratitude, 2) praise, and 3) a memory trigger. First, I thanked them for taking the time to talk with me. Second, I offered some nugget of praise for their character (it helped that I met three men who had stellar reputations in the League). If this was not the case, then I would have offered some praise for the way their particular position groups played in the matchup. And finally, I added a memory trigger. This was the most important aspect of the note, in my opinion. I understood that coaches were busy people and met a variety of people each week. I also knew they were generally sleep deprived and very short on leisure time. Any small mention to help them remember me would work in my favor. Although our pregame encounters were monumental to me, I wasn't arrogant enough to think that the meeting significantly altered a coach's day.

I was playing the long game—that introduction and my reachback note would be the first two salvos I would wage in the war of relationship building. Over time, my goal was to build a base of recognition and friendship that would help me cultivate my coaching skills and employment prospects. In a profession that functioned through referrals and endorsements, I wanted to build an army of coaches who could vouch for my coaching skills as well as my character. I imagined coaches who were looking to hire other coaches calling up their comrades to ask, "What do you know about this guy?" It was important that the background check yielded solid and personal recommendations.

For my next task, I turned to my computer. I created a spreadsheet especially for maintaining my coaching contacts. I entered the name of each coach that I had met in one column. Then I documented the date and three nuggets from our encounter in the next two columns. In the last two columns, I included the date that I mailed the letter and noted whether I received a response.

After placing stamps on the letters, I went to the outgoing mail bin and lifted out all of the mail that had not yet been picked up and placed my letters underneath the pile. While I was generally impervious to what other people thought of me, I was acutely aware of the current environment. We were winless and had just suffered a tough loss at Chicago; I didn't want to create any suspicions that I was consorting with the enemy. Stashing my letters near the bottom of the pile would conceal my efforts.

In the short time it took to write the letters, the coffee had brewed. I poured a cup and repeated my tasks from the previous Sunday night. What I saw on the big screen was worse than it had looked in real life. Going into the game, Prief had stressed that we were not going to let Devin Hester beat us single-handedly. Well, he had come quite close. On the punt return that he took for a seventy-three-yard touchdown, the tape showed a comedy of errors. Hester caught the ball at the twenty-seven-yard line, faked to his right, dodged two defenders, and tightroped his way along the left sideline. That Hester was notorious for embarrassing teams and creating instant ESPN highlight reels was not comforting in the least. The tape also showed that a few Chiefs players had been completely dominated by Chicago blockers on the play. We lost nearly every one-on-one matchup, and it was ugly.

The next thing that jumped off the projector screen was our lack of "backside pursuit." Backside pursuit is coach-speak for "hustle." Simply put, are players who seem to be out of the play (that is, because they are too far away) still running with the intensity of someone who is able to affect the action? The game of football mirrors life in so many ways, including instances where oftentimes the action seems far away and outside the realm of our control. But what separates the living from the dead is a willingness and determination to keep chasing in spite of distance or time. Our overwhelming biological urge is to conserve energy, so if a play seems out of one's control, most players will decelerate because they don't think they have a chance to affect the play. These types of people don't last very long in the NFL. And in life, "play it safe" types of people don't achieve very much.

As I began filling in my grade sheet, I noticed there were more minuses this week than there were for the previous game. Sure, we had scored more points, but our energy level looked even worse. Players were slow to respond. The split second of difference in our reaction time and our opponent's was just what the other team needed to get the best of us.

I completed my special teams grades faster than the previous week—I was getting better and my diagnosis time was getting shorter. When I first started reviewing film in July, I would have to repeat a play twenty to thirty times. It would take a long time for my vision to sharpen enough to distinguish the twenty-two players in the massive blur. I remember Gibby noticing this one day. He watched from the doorway as I hit the rewind button over and over and over. His advice: "D, just follow the ball. Find the ball first, and then everything else will clear up. Go to the ball."

I nodded in understanding, but inwardly I was rolling my eyes. What kind of advice is "Follow the ball"? Of course I was trying to follow the damn ball! But with twenty-two of the world's fastest and most powerful human beings running around in 57,600 square feet of real estate, it felt nearly impossible to locate. I cursed Gibby for all of his years of college playing experience and his tutoring as the son of an NFL coach. That he thought something as trite as "Follow the ball" would work for me made me want to throw the computer monitor at him.

On this Monday after the second game of the season, however, I realized his KISS advice, although frustrating at the time, had yielded results. My eyes had sharpened on the ball with laser focus. And I noticed that I didn't have to keep looking down at the remote to locate the rewind and fast-forward buttons. With the dexterity and muscle memory of an adolescent video game junkie, I instinctively hit the proper keys. In just a brief scan of the play, I could locate the problem area, zoom in on the action, and pinpoint who the likely offenders were.

After finishing special teams, I checked my watch—it was 1:30 a.m. My Coleman mattress beckoned me from the underbelly of Arrowhead, but I resisted. I made another pot of coffee and broke into a box of Pop-Tarts. I was going to work straight through and move on to defense. Grading the defensive tape would take at least four hours *and* no one but me would see my results.

Getting some sleep could help me be more productive the rest of the day, but I couldn't do it. I had a streak to maintain. This would be the second consecutive week that I had completed the grading the same day of the game. I could do it. I pressed Play. Looking back at that decision point, I realize how important the decision to keep my routine was. No one was watching me. No one was checking my work. No one would yell at me if I didn't submit my weekly grades. All of those reasons would have been convenient excuses for me to invoke in choosing sleep over sacrifice. But to get that contract and become a coach in the NFL, that approach was not going to work. I had to stay on the grind.

# THE GRIND

"D! Get up!"

As I came to consciousness, I was cognizant of the fact that I was experiencing one of my worst fears—being awakened by Herm or another coach as I was lying in drool-covered sheets of paper.

I fought the impulse to jump and feigned grogginess as I tried to figure out who was poking me. It was the security guard.

"Thanks. What time is it?"

"Damn, man, it's 4:15. I'm telling you something, and I know you're not going to listen to me, but if you keep going at this pace, we are going to be throwing your ass in a coffin. You know what happened to Vermeil."

He was alluding to the infamous breakdown of Dick Vermeil. The former Philadelphia Eagles head coach had suffered a mental break-down after the 1982 season. I remembered reading that Vermeil had said he drove into work one day, parked, and just couldn't get out of the car. The emotional and physical wear of the season had worn him out to the point that he couldn't muster the energy to simply walk into the building. That was a pivotal moment in the profession. Before Vermeil talked about his difficulty in maintaining the frenetic pace of the business, coaches adhered to a strict, unspoken code of conduct called "grinding."

The commitment to the grind was imparted through iconic coaches like Paul Brown and Vince Lombardi, men who would spend endless hours in the office and who expected the same from their assistants. The running joke in the NFL was that every team had a "lookout guy" whose job it was to alert the coordinators when the head coach left the building for the night. When the coordinators left, the lookout guy alerted the position coaches, and so on, until he was the only one left in the building. Vermeil's breakdown exposed the culture of the grind and loosened it up slightly. But as evidenced by my early morning wake-up call, some of us still found it to be a necessary practice to climb the profession's ladder.

■ ■ ■

With the rise of analytics in sports, technological advances in number crunching and video systems started creeping into the world of football. One touted benefit of adding these analytical tools was efficiency. Of the three major American sports, baseball had been the first to fully embrace analytics, and the practice had next migrated into professional basketball. Football was the final frontier for accumulating as much data as possible on players, plays, and team tendencies, and the computer counterintelligence war was just revving up during my time with the Chiefs.

The rise of analytics resulted in a battle that had no end. The more data that teams started to collect on opponents, the more nuanced scouting reports became. The information overload seemed like a good thing, until of course it became a bad thing. One example illustrated the point—the Chiefs' defensive scouting report for each week's opponent numbered more than two hundred pages. Most of those pages were packed with complex statistics that illustrated trends for a myriad of in-game scenarios. First down, third down, and red zone were just a few of the data buckets in the scouting reports.

The digital arms race by every team in the League resulted in a stalemate of new knowledge and a resurgence of the grind. Each team knew that the other team knew exactly what its tendencies were. And so what was the response? The number of "tendency breakers" spiked as coordinators tried to outsmart their counterparts. Assistants slaved away on their computers to find the next nugget of numerical data that could help create an advantage in the upcoming matchup. So much for efficiency.

As Herm would say, "You are who you are." Eventually, teams would resort back to the tried and true, both on the field and in the office. For me, a grunt ~~at the bottom of~~ beneath the totem pole, my job was to do what I was told, and then some. I concentrated on looking at and listening to what was going on around me. And by "listening," I don't mean "waiting to talk." Since I was never called on in meetings, I absorbed every piece of hard and soft data that bounced off the walls of our meeting rooms. It was an education unlike any other.

From my spot in the back of the room, I noticed the effect that "grinding" had on the assistant coaches. Most of them were married and many of them had school-aged children. Although Herm encouraged coaches to attend dance recitals and basketball games, the reality was that coaches were committed to their craft to such a degree that many times they chose football over family. Coaches would spend as much time as they deemed necessary to prepare for a game. Each week's matchup was another very public bullet point on their résumé. Sport is one of the professions with the unfortunate distinction of broadcasting regular global updates on one's job performance. If an accountant makes a miscalculation in an audit, a few people may find out; if a quarterback makes an error, millions of people see it in real time and have access to it in perpetuity.

As I gathered my papers early that morning, I saw Gun walking into the office. He looked at me, looked past me, walked into his office, and slammed the door. It would be a long day.

## THE RIGHT MINDSET

In this hyperbolic equation of football, Herm was a constant. He asked the same questions as the week before. What did your unit do well? What did your unit not do well? What is your plan to get better? Each coach gave a report on the previous day's performance with an eye to improving in the next week of practice. Although we were only in week three of the season, I could sense the weight of monotony in the process.

"We're doing this again?" I wondered to myself. While the methodology could be useful, the one-size-fits-all approach of Herm's system was making me anxious. Could we alter our output in the upcoming week without altering our analysis of what had gone wrong?

And then my anxiety became embarrassment. I began to feel guilty for letting a couple of losses alter my trust. What we were experiencing in the dank environs of a conference room was the part of the NFL that the fans would never see. Yet I was experiencing it firsthand. If I wanted the euphoria of working the sidelines of an NFL game and experiencing the glory of a team victory, this was a necessary step in my initiation.

Herm's voice pulled me out of the cooler of self-pity that I had built for myself. His message to the coaches felt like it was directed right at me.

"Remember, guys, we must create the mindset for this team. Some of our players will look for ways to dodge the work. Make sure you create the right mindset in your room."

Everyone scribbled the reminder into their notebooks and the meeting was adjourned.

After the day's meetings were over, Herm walked into the press box and said, "Come see me for a minute, D, I got something I want you to look at."

I almost choked. "Yes, sir," I blurted out, as I grabbed my notebook and a couple of pens and followed him into his office.

He turned to his computer and clicked on a cutup. "Have a seat," he said as he nodded across his desk.

I sat down and opened my notebook. I wasn't sure what was about to happen, but my inner voice told me to do one thing: focus. I didn't want to have to ask for any points of clarification after the meeting unless I absolutely needed to clear something up.

"I need you to go through all of the Oklahoma games that Adrian Peterson played in and put together a cutup. This guy, Peterson, he's a good back, but I keep hearing he had a fumbling problem in college. I need you to go find all of his fumbles in college. I want to take a look at them."

Adrian Peterson was college's best running back the previous season. Our only chance of winning would be to limit his production.

"When do you need the cutup, Coach?" I asked.

"As soon as you can get it to me. Players are back on Wednesday. Get it to me Wednesday or Thursday," he said.

I scribbled the notes down in my notebook:

- Adrian Peterson
- All seasons @ OU
- Cutup of ALL fumbles
- Due: WEDNESDAY OR THURSDAY

"I'll jump on this right now," I said.

As I walked out of his office, I noticed my sweaty palms had left imprints on my notebook sheet. I was nervous and excited at the same time. This was my first real assignment from the head coach.

I walked right into Gibby's office. He was watching Vikings film.

"Gibby, I need some help."

"Yep," he said, never taking his eyes away from the screen.

"Herm wants me to make a cutup of Peterson's fumbles from college."

"Okay," Gibby said. "You need to hit up the video guys. They can tell you how to pull up college tape. That project is going to take a while. When does he want it?"

"He said Wednesday or Thursday."

"Well, why you still standing here?"

"Good point. Thanks for the tip."

I walked straight to the video office. The room was like mission control in a contemporary war movie. There were flashing lights everywhere, and multiple screens showed football plays moving at every possible speed.

The video department is the main artery of every NFL team. Given that video is the lifeblood of player evaluation, the video staff held the keys to the kingdom. Each Tuesday, they would upload every play for every NFL game that had been played that week. The video team uploaded the footage in real time so that coaches, players, and scouts could consume tape upon demand.

The team had scouts on the road scouring the earth for college talent. There were scouts in the building evaluating every player on every team on every single play. These scouts generated a "ready list" for potential trades and acquisitions. Then there were high-level members of the Chiefs brass—the president, general manager, and owner—who would need any-time access to film. Meeting the needs of coaches, players, and staff (many of whom had personal video stations in their homes) made for a busy and stressful environment in the video department.

As I walked in, Director of Video Operations Pat Brazil was throwing an expletive up against the wall. "Damnit!" he yelled. So I turned to Ken Radino, one of his trusty assistants.

"Is this a bad time?" I asked.

"It depends. Are you here delivering cookies, or do you need something?" he replied.

I was sure he was only kidding, but his comment made me even more nervous. "Herm gave this project to me a few minutes ago and I need to jump on it."

Ken perked up a bit. "What is it?" he asked.

"He wants me to pull Adrian Peterson tape from Oklahoma and make a cutup of his fumbles," I said.

"Okay, that could get tricky. You gotta talk to Pat. College tape is a whole 'nother animal."

I tentatively approached Pat. His eyes were darting between multiple screens with the precision of a sniper.

"So . . . Herm wants me to work on this project. He wants me to make a cutup of all of Adrian Peterson's fumbles from his last year at Oklahoma," I said.

"When does he want it?" Pat asked.

"He wants it Wednesday or Thursday," I said.

"Which really means he wants it Tuesday," we both said in unison.

Pat and I both knew that Herm was just being kind with his deadline. He really needed it as soon as humanly possible. Tuesday meant I needed to turn it in in less than twenty-four hours.

"What will it take to get the college footage?" I asked.

"Well, give me a couple of hours, D. I can get some of these machines going right now. Then we can get you set up on a machine downstairs," Pat said.

"Thanks, Pat, I appreciate it."

I left the office and went straight to the press box. Luckily, I had gotten ahead on my work for Prief, and I only had a little bit to do to finish up my research on the Vikings. I started to map out my strategy for Operation Fumble-itis.

What would be the most time-consuming part of this project? That was simple: finding the fumbles. Generally, college football games operated at a faster pace than NFL games, and so there were roughly twenty more offensive plays per game in a college match. If I could identify the specific games in which Peterson fumbled, I could greatly reduce the time I would spend in going through every game.

I went to the most reliable database that I could find: Google. After a few dead-end searches, I finally found what I was looking for. Over the course of three seasons, I found the Sooners' game schedules.

Then I searched for fumbles each week of the season. In total, Peterson had made seventeen fumbles in his tenure at Oklahoma.

Then I moved on to his draft reports. A few things jumped out at me. The football pundits thought Peterson would be a great running back at the pro level. Everyone compared him to Eric Dickerson, a Hall of Famer who employed the same upright running style that Peterson used. In Peterson's "Weaknesses" column, however, the first thing that observers mentioned was a tendency to carry the ball loosely. It's no wonder he had a high fumble rate, and Herm was counting on this to be the Vikings' Achilles' heel. In a game where even one additional possession could give you a significant edge on an opponent, being able to create and capitalize on turnovers was critical.

After taking note of each game that Peterson had fumbled in, I got a call from Pat. "Hey, man, your video is ready. I just put it into the system. Let me know if you can't find it."

It didn't take me long to locate the film. I sat in front of the screen, cracked a Red Bull, pressed the Play button, and went to work.[21] Nearly six hours later, I was done. I had worked smarter, not harder. At least I hoped I was done. I double-checked, triple-checked, and quadruple-checked my work. I was certain that I had every Peterson fumble in my cutup.

The following day, I circled Herm's office, waiting for just the right time to let him know that I had finished the project. A procession of scouts and coaches prevented me from talking to him before noon. Finally, after lunch, I saw my opening.

---

21    I know you are starting to think that the Red Bull references are examples of some conspicuous product placement. This is not true.

"Coach, I got that cutup done for you."

"What?" Herm said. I couldn't tell whether he couldn't remember what he had asked me to do or he was surprised that I had completed it so quickly.

"The Peterson fumbles," I reminded him.

"Yeah, wait, you're already done with it?"

"Yes, sir," I said.

"Well, let's look at it," he said. "Come over here to my computer and pull it up."

In my planning for notifying Herm of completing my project, I had guessed there could be a very slight chance that he would ask me to watch it with him. So, before I left my office, I had emailed a copy of the cutup to both of us.

I clicked on the reel, Herm took the remote, and we watched.

"You see that, D? You see the way he holds the ball? He pumps his arms and sometimes the ball gets away from his body. That could be big for us. Good work, D. I didn't think you'd get it done so quickly. I hope you didn't spend too much time on it," he said.

"No, sir. I just decided to go ahead and jump on it," I lied.

"Well, good work."

As I exited Herm's office, I felt like I had just won the lottery. My first project for him had gone well. I was so excited, I needed to share it with someone. I walked back to Gibby's office. As usual, he was watching tape.

"I just finished that project for Herm. We watched the cutup. He liked it," I said.

"Wait." Gibby held up a "one sec" finger. "You're already done with it?"

"Yep, just showed it to him."

"Well, you screwed that up."

"What do you mean?"

"Now, he's going to expect you to finish every project that fast. You gotta do a better job of managing expectations."

I walked out of his office. Although ninety-eight percent of what Gibby had told me up until now had been sound advice, I quickly placed this latest nugget in the Out box. Gibby was sitting in the seat that I wanted. He had the luxury of being picky with the timing of his work submissions. I didn't. I wanted to make a positive impression on Herm. Now was not the time to be managing expectations. Now was the moment to be distinguishing myself as an indispensable asset.

■ ■ ■

At the Wednesday team meeting, Herm talked about the importance of creating a home-field advantage for the rest of the season. The Vikings match would be our first regular-season game at Arrowhead—a stadium known for being one of the loudest venues to play in professional sports. As Herm started to talk about the Vikings, he mentioned my cutup.

"I've looked at every fumble [Peterson] made in college. He carries the ball loose. He will put the ball on the ground. We have to create turnovers."

Although Herm never mentioned my name, I was ecstatic. I had just given the head coach a piece of information that was critical enough to mention to the whole team. This was all the acknowledgment that I needed. Of course I would have loved for Herm to have given me credit for my work, but I realized that saying my name wouldn't have changed my contribution.[22] The head coach appreciated my work. That was all that I needed.

As the week accelerated toward the Vikings matchup, the tension in the building was palpable. What would happen if we had another loss? Would Herm need to shake up his coaching staff to turn the team around? Would the organization start looking at potential coaching replacements? Each year, firings of head coaches seemed to occur earlier and earlier in a season. This game could be the turning point or cliff dive to our season.

## PIVOT POINTS

1   Reach back to new contacts within twenty-four hours of your encounter.

2   Add more to your plate. Then add some more. You can handle more than you think.

3   Maintain relentless "backside pursuit." Even the goals that seem unattainable now will come into focus if you keep chasing them.

4   Keep your eyes on the ball. Don't let the chaos around your goals distract you.

---

22   I did have a dream the night before the team meeting. Herm turns to me and says, "Rise, Daron." The room goes dark and a single beam of light illuminates my face. The head coach goes on to praise me incessantly.

5   Study your own tendencies more than you study the
tendencies of your opponent.

6   Underpromise. Overdeliver. Ask for more.

7   Create value instead of looking for credit.

# CHAPTER 8

# DON'T GET TOO HIGH

The euphoria from our Vikings win was palpable. It felt as if we had won the Super Bowl. The tremor of 78,038 fans filling the seats in Arrowhead had sent shock waves through my body and it felt good. The team had played like a group of resurrected men. They started fast and finished fast, just like Herm had demanded.

And just like that, it was over. Without family or friends in Kansas City, I could either retire to my Coleman or keep the celebration going on my own. So I decided to head to LC's, my favorite barbecue place in the city. LC's was a classic establishment. I had only recently learned about LC's, having been sent there on a lunch run by Bernard Pollard, one of our safeties.[23]

He turned to me after practice one day and said, "D, I ordered some sandwiches for the DBs for lunch, go pick it up."

"Where?" I asked.

"LC's," he said. "You know where that is?"

"No doubt," I bluffed as he handed me two hundred-dollar bills and walked off.

I didn't even shower. I bolted straight for the parking lot. Then I remembered: I had absolutely no clue where LC's was.

I stopped by the security guard's shop.

"Hey, man. I need a favor. Where in the hell is LC's?" I asked.

The security guard started telling me a story about the last time he had been there and how juicy the ribs were. As he droned on and on, all I could see was the clock over his left shoulder. I had forty-seven minutes before I was expected back with lunch. I had to get back to Arrowhead with enough time to get the food to the guys so they could inhale it before Gibby's defensive backs meeting began. He had a strict no-food policy. Eat in the meeting, get fined. Arrive late to the meeting, get fined. I was in a race against time.

"I kinda need to get there now. You mind telling me how to get there?" I interjected.

His directions were almost as convoluted as his story about the ribs. Nevertheless, I scribbled them down in my pocket notebook. It

---

23    If you take a trip to Kansas City and ask locals for barbecue-joint advice, you will get a range of suggestions—Arthur Bryant's, Jack Stack, and Gates, to name a few. Disregard all of this nonsense and go to LC's. If you are not pleased with your dining experience, send your receipt to me and I will reimburse you for your troubles.

was 2007 so I didn't have Google Maps on my phone (I couldn't even access the Internet on my phone). I jumped in my truck, ripped the sheet of directions from my notebook, and screeched out of the lot.

The beginning of the trip did not look promising, but I made it to LC's, a dusty brown building nearly indistinguishable from the surrounding nondescript buildings and landscape. You had to *intend* to find LC's, you didn't just end up there. I jumped out, ran in, got the order, and zipped back to the stadium.

My Tahoe was filled with the fumes of slow-cooked, smoky meat. From the look of the receipt, Bernard had chosen just about every conceivable option on the menu. There were ham and brisket, ham and sausage, and brisket and sausage sandwiches, just to name a few. The side of choice was home-cut fries that looked to be heavy enough to double as a small dumbbell.

As I drove into the lot, my empty belly began to get the better of my brain: *Just take a fry. Consider it your delivery fee.* I was starving and really wanted to swipe a few, but I just couldn't do it.

As I walked into the lunchroom, a few offensive linemen stopped me in the hallway, obviously drawn to the contents of the greasy brown bags.

"Who are those for, D?"

"What?" I responded. I knew exactly what was happening and I was buying a little more time. There were seven hundred pounds standing between me and completing my mission and I was not about to get frisked this close to my goal.

I needed to come up with something quickly. "Uh, these are for Herm and the rest of the coaches."

That was it, my trump card. Of course I was lying, but this was an emergency. Offensive linemen shared the top rung of the food chain on our team with defensive linemen. They possessed a lethal combination of size and a general disregard for the welfare of others. They were the biggest and generally the most capricious guys on the team. If there was a fight at practice, there was a ninety percent chance it was between offensive and defensive linemen, and unless someone (usually other linemen) broke up the fights quickly they could spiral out of control.

The guys were trying to figure out if I was telling the truth. I looked both of them in the eyes.

"Whatever." They shrugged and let me go.

I walked into the cafeteria, dropped the bags on the table in front of Bernard, and took the change out of my pocket.

"Don't worry about it, D. Keep the change, bro."

. . .

It was that seventy-five dollars that I was going to use to buy a brisket sandwich that Sunday night in celebration of our first regular-season win. Or so I thought. The place was closed. The one time I decided to treat myself, the only place where I wanted to eat was closed. So I changed course and stopped for a six-pack of Boulevard beer, Kansas City's finest beverage, and headed back to Arrowhead. I figured I could make a few peanut butter and jelly sandwiches for dinner and watch all of the plays from the Vikings game as an uninterrupted reel. Usually, I replayed each play over and over, looking closely for some minute detail. In celebration of the whole team's hard work, I was going to watch the entire game without any interruption.

Since I was also going to be drinking alcohol, I decided to move from my normal video-watching digs to another location. I wrapped each bottle of Boulevard in a pair of sweats (to avoid the giveaway clinking sound), threw all of them into a Reebok duffle bag, and walked nonchalantly through the front door. I nodded to the security guard and then made my way to the offensive line's room.

As soon as I sat down and opened a bottle, I took a few minutes to reflect on how far I had come. I had just played a small role in an NFL victory. None of my contributions would show up in the stats box in the paper the following day or get mentioned on *SportsCenter* that night, but the feeling of being a part of a victory was exhilarating. For a brief moment, the sleep deprivation, sweaty days of practice, and ridicule from my law school classmates was worth it. I thought of the perennial winners in the NFL. The Patriots and Colts came to mind. Could winning ever get old for those teams? When I looked at it in the context of all the work we had put in to win a single game, I had my answer. You expended so much energy for one victory— there was no way anyone could take this feeling for granted.

As I watched our players zip across the screen during the first half, it looked as if we might be headed for 0–3. We were making fewer mental mistakes than we had made in previous games, but we were getting "outmanned"—losing the one-on-one matchups. Adrian Peterson was running over, around, and through us, and our offense was faltering to the point of embarrassment. And then something changed in the second half. We looked like an entirely different team. I couldn't recall exactly what Herm had said in the locker room at halftime, but I could remember that it had looked like a triage unit with guys getting IVs, throwing helmets, and getting yelled at by their position coaches.

But whatever had happened in that locker room—whether it was Herm's speech, self-injections of pride, or a combination of both—it had worked. We came out of the tunnel with guns blazing. Realizing that we would not be able to run the ball against a stout Minnesota defense, the second half featured a complete air assault, and it worked.

After a ~~couple~~ few beers and finishing the tape, I decided to fill out my grade sheets. As I started to run the copies, I took a look back at the grades I wrote from the first two weeks and compared them with the coaches' grades. With each week, the separation between my grades and the coaches' grades grew narrower. I finished my sheets and headed to my "room." For the first time in three months I was looking forward to seven hours of sleep. The Coleman blow-up would feel like a king-sized bed at the Four Seasons.

## ON A ROLL

Our coaches' meeting the next morning had a distinctive air to it. There was more oxygen in the room. Guys seemed more relaxed and Herm's roll call of coaches' reports didn't sound like the call of the executioner.

As the fly on the wall, I took note of the marked difference in body language. Guys smiled more. There was more small talk during the downtimes in discussion.

Herm finished the meeting with a surprising reminder: "Okay, we're getting close to the twenty-four-hour deadline for moving on. Let's let these guys feel good about the win yesterday, but coach them hard in your meeting rooms. I want them to know how to improve, and I want it to be specific. Tell them exactly what they need to do to get better. And don't let them celebrate this win after today. You guys know this, but some of the rookies don't. The season is a marathon, not a sprint." And with that, we swept up the confetti, put the corks back in the champagne bottles, and went back to work.

▪ ▪ ▪

The next four weeks passed in a blur. We built some momentum from the Minnesota win and went on a "run" of wins. The performances in our 3–1 run were a far cry from the production we gave in the first two weeks. Within a four-week span, our rookies stepped up to contribute at a high rate, veterans exerted their leadership in the locker room, and the coaching staff stuck together.

We weren't thrashing teams in our wins, but we were finding ways to squeeze out narrow victories at home and on the road. After beating the Chargers in San Diego (30–16), we lost by a narrow margin to the Jaguars (17–7) but rebounded with wins against Cincinnati (27–20) and the Raiders (12–10), our divisional rivals.

The Raiders, the project of NFL titan Al Davis, have been the Chiefs' archrival since the 1960s, when the two teams were birthed in the American Football League. After the NFL merger, the teams became division rivals in the AFC West. This matchup had featured some bloody duels, and regardless of the ups and downs of one team's talent level, the annual games were guaranteed entertainment. In the 2006 matchup, we won by two points in the most hostile sports environment I had ever witnessed.[24]

---

24    Gun, a coach who once worked for and was fired by Al Davis, would say, "This ain't college. In professional football, a win is a win." By that, he meant that style points didn't help an NFL team like they do in college football. The coaches and sportswriters who issued weekly votes oftentimes awarded additional points for a college team that had demolished its opponent. In the NFL, there was no such bump. You either won or lost. Period.

Still, there were troubling signs of weakness in our four-game run. Offensively, our production was barely sputtering along. We were "manufacturing" points and it was clear we didn't have the personnel to make a serious push in the second half. We were averaging just over 14.5 points per game. I was curious to see how this compared with production from the previous year. The team had posted close to twenty points per game in the previous season and it had been good enough to earn the Chiefs a playoff spot.

"Maybe this isn't so bad," I thought, checking myself. Then it hit me. Our current production level would put us at the thirty-first spot the previous year with just one team below us: the Raiders.

I tried to focus on the good signs. Our defense was only allowing opponents to score an average of 16.1 points per game. That had been good enough to put us at the second-best spot the previous year. If we could continue the trend, then we might have a chance to finish the rest of the season on a high note. It was too early to even utter the "p" word (playoffs), but everyone was thinking about it. Well, at least I assumed everyone else was thinking about it. I sure was. The idea of going to the playoffs in my first NFL season would be more than I could have hoped for. With nine games left, I was just scratching the surface. But in my mind, I was in the postseason.

## THE BYE WEEK

Herm didn't share my same "forward-looking" outlook. As we reached our bye week, everyone in the building was ready for a break. That is, everyone but Herm.

In 1990, the NFL introduced the "bye week" into its fall schedule. In a sport that featured a season nearly twice as long as the college season but with only half the roster size of college teams, the break—really a forced reset—was greeted with much anticipation from coaches and players alike. The typical bye week included practices until Wednesday or Thursday and then a long weekend off before returning to practice the following week. In the coaches' meeting before our bye, Herm seemed like a reluctant father discussing a curfew extension for his teenaged child.

"Now, we have to remember that a lot of these guys are going to go home and get around some people who don't have their best interests in mind. I'm going to tell them today to be careful, but I want all of you coaches to do the same thing. We still have nine games to go, and we all know that this season could go down the tubes if we don't come back in the right frame of mind."

And with that, the bye week began. As soon as I caught a whiff that the bye week would enable me to get back to Mount Pleasant, I started making plans. I called my mom.

"Mom, I need a home-cooked meal," I whispered.

"You want me to send it to the stadium?" she asked. My mom had been vigilant in fulfilling my orders in the past. She had sent countless pound cakes and other assorted goodies to Arrowhead for me to consume. At one point, the mail guy said, "Man, I can smell the damn cake through the box. I'm going to start taking a slice or two as a delivery tax."

"No, Mom, I'm coming home at some point on Thursday," I said.

"That's good, honey. When will you get here?" she asked.

"I'm not sure," I whispered, "I'm going to wait until the last coach leaves the building and then I'll head south. It should take me about six hours."

"Six hours? Not that quick, right?"

"I'm going to push it on the Indian Nation Turnpike," I said.

"Don't drive too fast, babe, we aren't going anywhere."

■ ■ ■

As soon as Herm adjourned the last meeting on Wednesday, I waited in the press box as the other coaches began to leave the building. My biggest concern was that Gun would stick around until midnight. The hardest-working man in the NFL, he could outlast anyone in the building if he wanted to. This was the one standoff that I did not care to win.

The entire offensive staff was gone, and most of the defensive guys had left too, but Gun's light was still on. I found every excuse to walk by his office. I refilled the drinks in the refrigerator. I reloaded the coffee cups in the cupboard. I filled every tray in the printer to the brim.

Finally, Gun came into the copy room and asked, "What are you still doing here?"

"Oh, just getting a little work done." I shrugged. Inside, I was praying to God that he would tell me he was about to leave the office.

"Got ya. I'm finally getting around to some work that I haven't been able to get done with all of these damn people around. This is the quietest time of the year." He smiled.

Inside I died a little bit. I saw my departure time fade into the horizon. I must not have hidden it well because Gun said, "D, get outta here. I know you're trying to stick around, but get outta here.

We got a long way to go until the end, and you gotta stay fresh if you're going to survive. I don't know where you're going, but go. I'm serious. You've done a good job. Now, get outta here."

By the time I stammered through a "Thanks, Gun, I really appreciate it," he was already gone, retreating back to the solitude of his video lair. I saw the door close and I bolted for the parking lot.

I had a full wardrobe at my parents' house, so there was no need for me to pack. I threw a couple of Chiefs caps and shirts for my family into my backpack and jumped in my Tahoe. It was 5:00 p.m. I could be home by midnight if I drove fast enough.

After a few hours on the road, two things became clear. First, this trip was going to take longer than six hours. I was just getting into Broken Arrow, Oklahoma, after three and a half hours of driving. Second, I would not be able to drive straight through. I could barely keep my eyes open. I pulled into a well-lit Exxon station, reclined my seat as far as it would go back, and took a snooze.

The blaring horn of an eighteen-wheeler truck shook me. As my pupils dilated in the bright sun, I tried to read my watch. It was 9 a.m.! How in the hell did I sleep for twelve hours in a parking lot? Every inch of my lower back felt like someone had peppered my backside with birdshot. As soon as I picked up my phone, I could see a scroll of missed calls from my mother. I called home. My dad answered.

"Dad, I'm fine, I pulled over for a quick snooze and it turned into a twelve-hour nap. Sorry. I'm in Broken Arrow; I should be home in four hours."

I walked into the Exxon and bought two Red Bulls and a travel-size toothbrush and toothpaste.

Four hours later, I was sitting at my dinner table with macaroni and cheese, baked chicken, candied yams, and collard greens set out before me. With the frenzy of a recently freed prisoner of war, I devoured everything. I couldn't stop. Each time I would pause and sit back for a sip of sweet tea, I'd think that I was done. And then the hunger would come back over me. I felt like I was somewhere between the continuum of a bear coming out of hibernation and one that was going back in. Not only was I making up for lost time, I was also storing up for the second half of the season. My parents and sister marveled at me with a mix of disgust and amazement on their faces. I was breaking every etiquette rule that Emily Post had ever written for the dinner table in the course of one meal. I was a man possessed.

And then I took a nap. And by nap, I mean another twelve-hour nap. When I awoke at midnight, my mom was waiting up, watching TV in the living room. I sat down on the couch and apologized. She understood. We talked about the grind of waking up before five and going to bed after eleven. The lack of sleep had caught up to me. I was making up for lost time. To be honest, the details of that bye week are still a blur to me. I felt like a patient going in and out of consciousness. But the time spent with family and the joy of seeing the piney woods of my youth were all that I needed to rejuvenate for the second half of the season.

On Saturday morning I gave my parents a hug, loaded my truck with a cooler of home-cooked food, and started the trip back to Kansas City. The return trip was not nearly as difficult. I arrived in KC close to sundown, refreshed and ready to tackle the rest of the season.

# THE ROOKIE WALL

Coaches began to trickle in on that Sunday to begin their preparations for the second run. I started to reconnect with the staff.

"Sax, how was the break?" I said as I walked into the coach's office. He was one of the best running back coaches in the League and, as an added bonus, he had also played the position for the Chiefs, so he was a fan favorite.

"Man, it was like nectar from the gods. A good recharge. I spent some time with the family. Actually, that reminds me. My son, Devin, has been getting some looks from different teams and it looks like Harvard is interested."

"Really?" I asked. "That's good stuff. What is he thinking?"

"Well, I think he likes the idea, but he's keeping options open. I say, if he can play there, then he needs to do it. Period. What do you think?"

"This is an easy one: He's gotta go to Harvard. Period. I would take that offer over any other school under the sun. Screw big-time college football. If he plays there, he will be set," I said.

"That's what I told him but, you know, he's a senior in high school and I'm his dad, which certifies me as an idiot," Sax said. We both chuckled.

"If you think it would help, I will talk to him. I will give him my 'soft sell.' I'm close to hitting thirty, though, so I'm sure he won't think I'm cool. But I will try."

"Appreciate that, D. Here's his number," Sax said.[25]

---

25    Devin chose Harvard. I take full credit for his decision.

"Okay, I will call him tonight," I said. "You ready for the second half of the season?"

Sax looked at me with a puzzled look. "Of course. I stay ready. But the question for you is, when are you gonna hit that rookie wall?"

"Rookie wall? Come on man, that's tooth fairy talk. I'm not hitting some rookie wall. I can grind all year."

Sax nearly fell out of his chair with laughter.

"Look, man, I played in this league for eight seasons and I've been coaching for eleven years. *Every* rookie hits a wall. I know you went to Haaaaaahvad, but that's not going to help you when you hit that wall."

The rookie wall was something that I had heard about since I started working with the team. It was one of those urban legends that offers a convenient explanation for the poor performance of a rookie. The theory behind it is that the first pro season—nearly twice as many games as college—is a psychological and physical nightmare for players just out of college. At some point in the season, a rookie hits "the wall." Common symptoms include lack of energy for workouts, inability to focus in meetings, and a general feeling of discomfort. Far from the euphoria of draft day, a rookie is confronted with the ugly side of surviving in the NFL ecosystem during the dog days of a season. For weeks on end, he is playing at the highest level of physical exertion that he has ever experienced, and most of the time it will feel as if he is gaining very little (if any) traction. This process is just like the labor pains experienced by the guy who is trying to jump from one career to the next one. At times, it seems as if there are rare moments of light. But the journey requires trust that continuing to march down the road will lead to a new life.

I dismissed Sax's comments. I was fine. I had just returned from an incredible seventy-two-hour binge of eating and sleeping. I was sure that the prolonged siesta was just what I needed to finish out the season.

Our post-bye-week opponent was Green Bay. It looked to be a real battle and we planned to hold our own. Green Bay had one of the top records at the time, as they had won six of seven games. They were undefeated on the road, and they had two veterans—Brett Favre and Charles Woodson—who were playing much better than their ages should have allowed. At the time, Favre and Woodson were thirty-eight and thirty-one. Those were ages at which most football players noticeably decline in their production and skills. These two Packers, however, were playing like invigorated rookies. They were the focal points of our preparation. The one stat in our favor was that Favre was winless (0–3) against Kansas City in his storied career. In fact, the Chiefs were the only team in the NFL that he had *not* beaten.

This game was special for me for another reason: It gave me the chance to reconnect with Mike McCarthy, the Packers' head coach. Before I started coaching, a mentor and good friend, Kent Lance, arranged a meeting between McCarthy and me in Austin. For two hours, I sat right across the table from one of the top coaches in the National Football League. He was tough and had clawed his way into the League from the college ranks. His team reflected his demeanor, playing with an intensity that was unrivaled in the NFL. During the usual pregame handshake period, I would make a point to reintroduce myself to McCarthy.

. . .

As we sat in the first players' meeting after the break, Herm's message was clear: It's time to get back to work. He stressed the importance of the strong "finish." The fact that we went into our bye week as divisional leaders meant absolutely nothing.

While the players seemed to transition back into our schedule without any hiccups, I could tell that something was off. Before the bye week, we were thriving on the energy of winning games and immediately preparing for the next matchup. Now, something felt off. And it wasn't just me. During practice on the Thursday of that week, I strolled up beside one of our equipment managers on the field and mumbled, "Is it just me or is something off here?"

He looked both ways to see if someone was within earshot of us and said, "It's not just you."

The following Sunday against the Packers was a disaster. We lost, 33–22. The play of the game typified the challenges we could not seem to overcome. With 3:05 remaining in the fourth quarter, we were ahead 22–16. If we could just keep them from scoring another touchdown, we would win and be 5–3. With Favre at the helm, the Packers threw a sixty-yard touchdown pass to score, taking the lead. They added a field goal, and then an interception return for another touchdown. It was an ugly defeat.

Unfortunately, our Packers loss set the stage for the rest of the season. Over the course of the next eight weeks, we went 0–8. We lost every single game after the bye week. It felt as if the entire team—vets included—had hit the rookie wall. The feeling inside Arrowhead grew more bleak as we limped through the final weeks of the season.

From the locker room to the community affairs office, everyone was deflated by our losses.

As I looked back over my high school playing career, I realized that I had never been on a losing team. In my last two years of high school football, we reached the semifinals and quarterfinals of the playoffs in back-to-back seasons. The feeling of despair in Arrowhead was something that I was not accustomed to. I did not handle the situation in the best way.

As I continued to work long hours, I wanted to show others that I was committed to the cause. I was too sensitive to what I thought others were thinking of me—that perhaps I was a moonlighting academic who couldn't handle the blunt force of a challenging NFL season. So I turned my gaze outward, looking for people whom I thought were "cutting corners." I loathed those who did not meet my personal commitment test. In an effort to deflect my own insecurities about the fate of my position on the team, I was judging others' commitment. This was not only unproductive, it was destructive. That was neither my responsibility nor should it have been my obsession. I should have used that energy to stay committed to improving my coaching skill set. I had reached the rookie wall that Sax had warned me about, and instead of trying to scale the obstacles and reach the other side, I leaned against it and turned my attention outward.

Perhaps you've been a part of an organization that suffers a losing streak—consecutive quarterly sales are on the decline or student test scores have dipped in back-to-back years—and you didn't handle the situation the right way. Maybe you felt like the losses justified your arriving to the office a little later than usual or, on the opposite end of the spectrum, maybe you started to judge the commitment of others without hearing their perspective. I believe these two reactions are common human tendencies. In the face of adversity, it becomes easy to cut corners or start to blame others.

Evaluating your team's roster is important, but the first question that must be answered is: How can *I* improve this company? How can *I* make this school better? If we are honest, our personal to-do list will be a long one. And the time that is needed for us to continue to improve our personal production and growth will leave little time for evaluating the commitment of others. Turning organizations around hinges on turning people around. Successful transition hinges on being honest about our personal faults and working consistently to create better versions of ourselves. That growth process allows us to make the personal transitions we seek.

Enduring a losing season was tough. With each week, the din from the sportswriters grew louder and louder. The pundits had so many pieces of advice, but they all had the same message: Fire Herm, fire Prief, fire the offensive coordinator. Better yet, fire everyone in the building and start from scratch. With Black Monday just around the corner, we braced for the executioner.

Black Monday—a play on Black Friday but not nearly as positive—is a term that has been used to describe the day on which most of the firings take place in the League. For an NFL owner, the sixteen-game season provides enough time to evaluate the performance of its coaching staff and roster. And so, on the Monday after the regular season ends, many owners place coaches on the chopping block.

We weren't all fired on Black Monday—Chiefs management waited until Tuesday. Our offensive coordinator, offensive line coach, wide receivers coach, and running backs coach (my good friend Sax) were the first to go. It happened so quickly; I was mesmerized by the process. Each coach had a scheduled meeting with Herm that morning. By the end of the day, their offices were cleaned out. It was gut-wrenching. These were guys that I had seen nearly every day for the past six months. If you added up the total hours spent together in the office, it was really more like we had worked the equivalent of a year together. And suddenly they were looking for jobs.

As I witnessed this process unfolding, I became antsy. I couldn't sit still in my press box. What would happen to me?

## PIVOT POINTS

1   Take time to celebrate the victories, but spend less time partying than you do preparing for the next fight.

2   There are times when you must "zoom out." Force yourself to get above the minutiae and take in the bigger picture.

3   Determine whether your quest is a marathon or a sprint. Then, hydrate accordingly.

4   Does your profession award style points? If so, go for the flair. If not, follow the words of Al Davis: "Just win, baby!"

5   Give yourself the gift of a "bye week." Take a step away from the grind, but don't get too far away.

6   Beware the "rookie wall." Don't fear it, but understand that your body and mind will become weary.

7   In times of crises, fix what you can before judging.

# CHAPTER 9

# BLACK MONDAY

Debbie, the Chiefs' administrative assistant, tapped me on the shoulder. I jumped. My back was to the door and I was staring into space. Actually, I was staring at the fifty-yard line of the field, wondering if this would be my last week in the NFL. In total, we lost six of the eight games we played at home. As Gun would say, "if you don't have a home-field advantage, you don't have a chance in this league." Your home field is home to your "twelfth man," the crowd. The crowd provides just the right amount of additional pressure—in the form of noise—a team needs to rattle opposing quarterbacks.

When I first arrived in Kansas City, a security guard caught me in a hall one night and went on a rant about Arrowhead being the loudest stadium in the world. He claimed that he was at a game in 1990 when the Chiefs were playing the Denver Broncos. With the Broncos backed up near their own end zone, the crowd reached a pitch that could be heard for miles around. The security guard claimed that Broncos quarterback John Elway spoke to a referee about the noise level after he was unable to execute a play. After listening to Elway, the referee said, "Any further crowd-noise problem will result in a charged timeout against Kansas City. Thank you for your cooperation."

When the guy told me that, I just nodded my head and smiled. I figured he was senile. Then, a Google search backed him up. I never would have guessed that a ref would ask the crowd to quiet down during a football game. A tennis match? Of course. But a football game? This was unbelievable. I went to bed that night with a new-found appreciation for the Chiefs' fan base.

So, as I was jolted back to reality, I turned to Debbie. "Excuse me?"

"Daron, Herm wants to see you," she said.

For a moment the world stopped. My breath accelerated as if I had just finished a marathon. My palms got sweaty and I couldn't seem to move from my chair.

"Me?" I stammered.

"Yes, Daron." Debbie was getting impatient. "He wants to meet with you today. I will come back and get you. Just wanted to give you a heads-up."

She turned to walk away.

"Wait, Debbie, you think I should put something together?" I asked.

She stared at me. "Like what?"

"I don't know, a recap of my year?" I asked.

"Sounds good to me. Honestly, I don't know what the meeting is going to be about. I just wanted to tell you so you wouldn't venture too far from the press box," she said.

Well, she didn't have to worry about that. Now that I knew I was on the docket, I wouldn't eat, use the restroom, or do anything that would take me more than five feet away from the press box.

As I sat there wondering what to do with myself, I realized I had a dilemma. I didn't want to talk to anyone about the meeting. If I was about to hear bad news, I didn't want other people to know that the firing line had extended down to the very bowels of the franchise.

Then, with a chuckle, I realized I couldn't get fired—I had never been hired. At the time, if you performed a Google search for "Daron Roberts" all you would find were some random articles about my time as student government president at the University of Texas. I was nowhere to be found on the Kansas City Chiefs' digital footprint. I wasn't listed on any websites. I was invisible. People inside the building knew me, but no one else in Chiefs Nation had a clue who I was.

The reality was that there were many Darons in the NFL. Each week, I met a guy who would be standing off to the side, holding a bag of footballs. Recognizing a fellow grunt, I'd sidle up to him and introduce myself. After a few minutes, the ice would melt and we'd be laughing about life at the bottom. One guy I met with the Raiders was convinced the head coach didn't know he existed. He would clean up the meeting rooms and pick up food for the coaches, but on paper, he didn't exist. I remember him saying, "If I died in my basement, it would take at least a month for somebody to find me." We chuckled, but we both knew there was a good chance that he was right.

Recognizing that the period of invisibility is an incredibly beneficial position for the grunt is the first element of survival. Many ex-players who were accustomed to being in the spotlight withered in the desert of anonymity once they started climbing the coaching ladder. No TV stations were calling for interviews. Now, they were spending endless hours watching film and drawing plays.

With this in mind, I emerged from my shock and started to jot down a plan. Fortunately, I had dedicated thirty minutes each week to updating my résumé. Some weeks it might take thirty seconds and other weeks it would take the full thirty minutes, but I made it a practice to update my résumé as I took on additional responsibilities or completed projects. Slowly but surely, my "coaching résumé" had grown.

I was driving stakes across the football-coaching landscape. I didn't know if my next job in football would be in community relations, on another football staff, or in the mail room, but I had to make sure I was attractive in any position I could find. To beef up the résumé, I put my liberal arts degree to work by creative engineering. For example, to describe my kitchen-stocking duties, I listed the responsibility as "operations assistant."[26]

So with a padded—but not inaccurate—résumé ready to go as Exhibit A, I moved on to Exhibit B: the interview packet. It was customary for coaches who were interviewing for coordinator or head coaching jobs to create an interview packet. I first read about these "mystery packages" when I researched the coaching profession before

---

26   I hear you judging me. Listen, I was not pulling a George O'Leary (the man who lasted five days as head coach of Notre Dame before it was discovered that he had fabricated lettering in three sports and had created a mythical graduate institution and bestowed a master's degree upon himself). My résumé entries were just artful descriptions—not lies.

training camp. Andy Reid, for his interview as head coach of the Philadelphia Eagles, was famous for creating the most extensive packet that had seen the light of day. According to urban legend, the owner of the Eagles told Reid—after just fifteen minutes of hearing his presentation—that he was hired.

Reid's response was, "Thanks, but I'd like to finish so you have a clear idea of my vision for this football team."

And with that, he continued to lay out every facet of his pending management structure. He laid out his first choices for assistant coaches, strength and conditioning coaches, and administrative assistants. He laid out the schedules for the entire preseason, regular season, and postseason. He discussed his disciplinary structure and even talked about the seating arrangement on the team plane. Of course, all of this intel is anecdotal, but the story was retold to me enough times that I started to contemplate exactly what my interview packet for a head coaching job would look like.

In a Microsoft Word file code-named "GITB" (Get in the Building), I laid out a core outline of nine areas:

1   Philosophy
2   Vision
3   Short-, Medium-, and Long-Term Goals
4   Organizational Chart
5   Offensive Mindset
6   Defensive Mindset
7   Special Teams Mindset
8   Player Evaluation
9   Crisis Management

Of course, some people would say that it was too early—way too early—for me to develop my beliefs in these areas. If Gun or Prief had seen my notes, I'm sure I would have been thrown into a den of ridicule, never to be heard from again. But every week, I added more of my ideas to this document, and the process of reflection helped me to create an outline for the interview packet I would present to Herm.

1    Overview

2    Special Assignments

3    Production

4    Next Steps

5    Résumé

In the Overview, I briefly described my arrival and work throughout the season. This was my elevator pitch. I crafted this part of the presentation assuming that Herm would only spend two minutes reviewing the first page. So my "story" was short and to the point.

The Special Assignments section was where I listed every project I had taken on, whether it was picking up a free agent from the airport or creating a scouting report on the Chargers. This section was long and detailed. My theory was that if the reader had gotten this far, then I had hooked him. I would show him just how valuable I was to as many departments in the building as possible.

This form of organizational anchoring is key. If you are in an ecosystem with several departments, and you have the latitude to work on various projects, then do it. The age of sitting in a silo and waiting for the promotion gods to sprinkle magic dust on your cubicle is over. Pitching oneself to as many departments and partners in the building as possible increases your overall value. Remember this: If you don't get promoted and you are the only one who is disappointed, then you haven't done enough.

I understand that we don't live in a blissful meritocracy, and sometimes things like skin color, gender, and sexual preference interfere with the evaluation process. But my tactic for overcoming that is simple: Make it very hard for the company to get rid of you or, even worse, fail to promote you. Lead the team in sales, ~~make the best PowerPoint presentations~~ create the best ideas, and bring in the most clients, so the decision becomes a monetary matter: "If we lose her, then we will lose money." Once that becomes the issue, you win.

Your work product should be so good, and your value should be so high, that even your colleagues make the case for your promotion. It is not enough to serve as your own advocate. In order to create leverage, you need the support of others. Thus, you're valued for benefiting people outside of your immediate surroundings. The ideal situation is to create a buzz that reverberates through break rooms and over midday lunches. "We need to find a way to keep her." "He's going to be key for us moving forward, we need to make sure he stays." These are examples of the comments that upper management needs to hear in order to pull the trigger on your advancement. While most people want to believe that performance reviews are the sacred ground for making decisions about employees, the reality is that these decisions are usually made long before the formal review takes place. A collective buzz of support is what you will need in order to make forward progress.

Since I had worked with five different divisions on the team, I hoped my cumulative value would buoy my chances of getting to hang around for another season. While I would have been fine to continue in the same capacity, I was eager to reach the next tier: a quality control position. The quality control position is the holy grail of entry-level coaching jobs, and a roll call of head coaches have gotten their start in the position. That's what I wanted.

I zipped through the last three sections by copy/pasting the production numbers for special teams and defense. I had done projects for both units, so I would take credit for a sliver of their success. Since the special teams numbers were worse than defense, I moved the defensive stats to the top and buried the other special teams data below. I wanted the top of every page to scream, "Hire This Guy." As the brother of a journalist, I understood the importance of placing compelling content "above the fold." As eyes start to wander from the top of a page to the bottom, the brain loses interest. I couldn't afford to have my stock take a hit.

Under my Next Steps section, I typed the most important words of the entire document, "Given the rich football experiences I have had over the course of the past six months, I am ready, willing, and able to assume a paid position as a defensive quality control assistant."

I performed one last spell-check and hit the Print button. I jumped from my chair and darted for the copy room. The last thing I wanted was to have another coach read my document. As I walked into the room, I found Gibby opening and closing cabinets.

"D, you know where the damn black Sharpies are?" Gibby asked. "We use black Sharpies more than any other thing in this building, and I can never find them. It's like looking for Waldo every time I need to get some Sharpies."

I just stood there. I could hear the words that were coming out of his mouth, but all I could think about was the printer a few feet away, spewing the most important document I had ever created in my life.

"Yeah, second drawer to your right," I said, hiding my tension.

"Thanks, D."

And then he walked out.

I grabbed my papers, slapped a plastic cover on the front, and bound it for presentation. I was ready.

# THE MEETING

At 11 a.m. I was starving. I didn't know if it was because it was time for lunch or because anxiety was eating away at the lining of my stomach. What I did know was that I wasn't going to leave my desk. When a mail runner stopped by, I grabbed him.

"Hey, man, do you mind grabbing me a couple of Gatorade bars from the equipment room?"

"What's wrong with your legs?" he asked.

"Hey, man, I can't leave my desk. I think I may have a meeting today so I kinda need to stick around," I said.

"Oh." His eyes relayed an understanding of what might be around the corner for me. "I got you, bro. I'll bring a few up here. Does the flavor matter?"

"Whatever you can get your hands on—I just need to eat. Period. I appreciate the help."

I sat back down and reviewed my packet. I reviewed it again and again. The clock struck 3 p.m. and not only had my Gatorade bars never appeared, I still hadn't heard from Debbie. I strolled by her office and made eye contact just in case she had forgotten to relay a message from me. She nodded and turned back to her computer.

Around 5 p.m., she walked into the press box.

"Well, Daron, looks like Herm is ready to see you."

"Okay." I grabbed my packet, a notebook, and two pens and headed for the door.

When I walked in, Herm was on the phone. Although I couldn't ascertain exactly who it was, I suspected it was a fellow coach at another team. They were talking about the "ugly side" of the business and the perils of having to play so many rookies. I took a seat across from the head coach and tried to look inconspicuous. We've all had that awkward moment when you're in the office of someone higher on the food chain, and that person is on the phone. You don't want to make eye contact because that would suggest you're eavesdropping. But you *are* eavesdropping because, well, you are sitting in that person's office.

Finally, Herm put the phone down and started shuffling a few papers.

"D, how you doing?" he asked.

I lied and said, "I'm doing well, Coach, just getting ready for the offseason reports." The more accurate response would have been "I'm about to pee my pants from anxiety." I folded my right leg over my left leg so I could bolt my legs together and conceal my shakes. I don't think it worked.

"Good. Hey, I wanted to talk with you about something. We really appreciate all that you've done this season. You've been a really big help. I still don't know why you wanted to do this, but you've been good."

At this point, I began having flashbacks to three years of rejection wait-list letters from Harvard. Then the avalanche of form letters from NFL teams fluttered through my brain. Herm's words were sounding like the damning words of gratitude ("We want to thank you for submitting an application, but . . .") that plague rejection letters. I was clutching my packet and getting ready to make my case.

"So, here's the thing, it looks like we're going to move Ketch to assistant linebackers and make you the defensive quality control assistant."

Silence.

"Sir?"

"Yes, D, we're going to make you the defensive quality control coach. Unless, of course, you don't want that."

I finally jerked free of my shock-induced paralysis.

"Yes, sir, Coach. I really appreciate this. I appreciate this a lot. I won't let you down. I promise you that."

"Well, good. Carl will talk to you about a contract and all the legal stuff. Welcome to the NFL."

I got up, shook his hand more times than I should have, and walked out the door. I walked down the couple of flights of stairs into the basement of Arrowhead. The place was dead. I walked into the defensive linemen's meeting room, dropped to my knees, and cried. I cried some more, and then I cried some more. Every time I tried to pull myself together, I thought about the nights I had spent on that blow-up mattress. There had been quite a few nights that I wanted to deflate that mattress, throw all of my stuff into my Tahoe, and drive back to Mount Pleasant. But I didn't. My faith and my pride had kept me from throwing in the towel.

I called my parents.

"Hey, D, how are you?" my mom asked.

"I'm good, Mama. They're going to hire me," I said.

"What? Wait, let me get your dad on the phone."

My dad picked up the phone and I repeated the news: "They're going to hire me."

Neither of them could believe it. Even as I uttered the words, I couldn't believe it. This was the moment I had envisioned since the days I worked at that football camp back in South Carolina. It was happening.

I sat on the floor and noticed that I had never given my packet to Herm. I ripped it up, threw it in the trash, and headed back upstairs. It was time to get back to work.

## PIVOT POINTS

1   Remember this: "It's not about you." Don't expect too much from the top when you're working on the ground floor.

2   Update your résumé in real time. The best opportunities are usually unexpected. Stay ready so you won't have to get ready.

3   It's never too early to form your coaching philosophy. One day you're the grunt and the next day you're the general manager.

4   Load the good stuff above the fold.

5   Overprepare for the big meeting. No one ever walked out of a meeting and said, "I wish I hadn't prepared so much."

# CHAPTER 10

# ON THE PAYROLL

It took two months, but I finally got my meeting with Carl Peterson in March 2008. As the Chiefs' general manager, Peterson executed all of the team contracts for coaches, players, and scouts. He had spent nearly twenty years as the team's general manager and was known around the League as a cerebral man. Moreover, he was rumored to negotiate with the precision of a CIA agent.

As I geared up for my contract negotiations, I went to Gibby, my reliable historian and chief strategist. I had heard many horror stories about Peterson, and I needed to get an accurate scouting report on him before I had my big meeting.

As always, he was watching film when I walked into his office.

"D! What's up, man? You look nervous."

"Well, I'm trying to get ready for this negotiation with Carl. I've been pulling all of my materials together and I need to get some advice from you."

"Hold on, back up. What's that word you used?"

"What?" I asked. I wasn't sure where he was going with this line of questioning. "What do you mean, Gibby?"

"You said, 'negotiation.'"

"Right, 'negotiation.'"

"Well, that's where you're wrong," Gibby said. "This isn't going to be a negotiation. You are going to walk into his office. He is going to slide a piece of paper across the desk. You are going to sign that piece of paper, shake his hand, and walk out. Save the law school routine. Sign the contract and get back to work."

I walked out of his office. I was upset. I had believed that this next step would be my official foray into big-time coaching. But no, I would still be a grunt, just a grunt with a (nonnegotiable) salary.

When I walked into Carl's office, it felt as if I had entered a side room in the Pro Football Hall of Fame. Pictures of him with Lamar Hunt, a founder of the American Football League and first owner of the Chiefs, adorned the room.

As I sat down, I clutched my interview packets. Carl gave me a look. Finally, he said, "So you really want to do this?"

I had heard this question countless times since I first made the decision to embark on a coaching career. Today, however, it felt different. My other inquisitors were family members, classmates, and generally meddlesome strangers. But now, the general manager of an NFL team was asking me.

I paused.

"Yes, this is what I want to do. I'm all in."

"Daron, you realize a career in law could take you in a lot of different directions, right? You're sure the NFL is for you?"

"There's no doubt in my mind. This is exactly what I want to do," I replied with an air of indignation. I was tired of answering this question. If I wanted to practice law, I would already have an office on the thirty-second floor of a high-rise in downtown Houston, slaving away on a pile of contracts. Instead, I wanted to sit in a windowless basement room, slaving away on a stack of game videos. This was the life I wanted.

"Okay, here's the deal," he said as he pushed the contract across the desk. Then he ran through the terms of the contract: two-year deal; $50,000 per year; two tickets to each of the games; playoff bonus; and a new office. Plus I would get health and the other assortment of benefits that most white-collar citizens had.

Most important to me in that moment, I'd be a member of the coaching staff.

"You understand that as a defensive quality control assistant, your job is to do whatever Gun needs you to do. He's your boss. From there you answer to the head coach," Carl said.

"I got it," I said. I stood up, we shook hands, and I was on my way. I had built up two months of anxiety over an event that lasted approximately seven minutes. The compensation was a third of what I would have made as a second-year corporate attorney, but I could enjoy one especially incredible perk: I could wear sweatpants, sneakers, and Dri-Fit shirts ninety-nine percent of the year. In my mind, that benefit alone was worth $25,000. Everything else was gravy.

It took me one day to return the contract.

"Here's the contract," I said, as I placed it on Carl's desk the next day.

He checked the signature page and said, "Good, your office should be set up by the end of the day. Someone from HR will contact you about the pension and insurance."

I walked out grinning from ear to ear and got back to work. I sent a few text messages and emails to friends with the same general message: "I'm on the payroll!"

Within three hours, I had a new office (it was, of course, the space of one of our fired coaches). I had a computer, keys to my door, and health insurance by noon. By 3 p.m., I had a parking spot. By 5 p.m., the media-relations staffer was sitting in my office getting material for my online bio.

"Okay, where else have you coached?"

"Nowhere," I said.

"Okay, where did you play?"

"Mount Pleasant High School. I was a strong safety."

"Where else?" he asked in a leading tone.

"That's it."

"Excuse me?"

"Yep, that's it. Mount Pleasant High School, I lettered twice and I was a first-team All-District strong safety. Put that in there."[27]

The guy stared at me blankly.

"Um, okay. Let me see what we can do with all of this info. I will let you know once the bio goes live."

---

27     And yes, you can view my award in the Mount Pleasant Tigers Hall of Honor. Email me at coachdkr@coachdkr.com for directions.

# THE ELEVATED GRUNT

With a nameplate on my door, a new computer, and a locker overflow-
ing with Chiefs gear, I was ready to begin my new role as a defensive
quality control assistant in my second season. The position was created in 1990 when Mike Holmgren of the San Francisco 49ers hired a
young coach named Jon Gruden. The era of football was shifting into
the digital age and Holmgren needed a tech-savvy young coach to
transfer the stacks and stacks of football diagrams stuffed in decaying
notebooks into computer drawings. Gruden was that young guy, and
he became the godfather of the quality control position. What started
as a Holmgren gap-filler position turned into a League staple, and by
2007, every team had one quality control assistant for offense and one
for defense.

The position also came with an obligation to serve as quasi–chief
of staff for the coordinator. As Gunther Cunningham's direct report,
I took all of my cues and assignments from him, with my primary
responsibility to create a "breakdown" of our opponents—every play
from the team's three most recent games. I compiled the statistics
into a scouting report that was distributed to the head coach, defensive coaching staff, and every defensive player. It was a detailed task,
akin to charting the conditions for a successful NASA launch. I would
spend the majority of my time compiling information over the course
of the season. Each week brought an additional layer of anxiety, as the
turnaround time for delivery was always six days. Gun was notorious
for wanting to stay ahead of the competition, so not only would I have
to prepare the upcoming opponent's scouting report by the time we
boarded the plane on Saturday, but I had to stay two weeks ahead of

the schedule. As soon as the game was over on Sunday afternoon, Gun would start looking at the scouting report for the upcoming opponent.

In addition to this responsibility, I would assist all of the defensive coaches with any special reports they needed. And then there were the remnants of my unpaid grunt days. I picked up meals, set up and collected cones during practice each day, and was on call for any random job that might arise. I still helped to stock the cafeteria. I still made runs to LC's Bar-B-Q for sandwiches. I was still the grunt. But now I was the grunt with a checking account in the black.

While most people saw this as an extremely stressful position—and they were right—it was a rare opportunity to get an inside look at NFL play-calling. The process of evaluating opponents was a 360-degree education. Not only was I responsible for researching and presenting every minute detail about any opponent we would face, but coaches also would ask me for random information on the spot.

"Hey, D, who is that safety from Cal that everybody is raving about?"

"Hey, D, what folder should I save my PowerPoint in so I can show it to my players in the meeting room?"

It felt as if I were a medical student in residency. I was on call at all times. To keep up with the coaches' insatiable appetite for information, I made daily check-ins to Yahoo Sports, ESPN, and many other sites to get "insider information." I paid for memberships to a host of sites in order to get access to any "scoop" that might give me an edge. I had done this before I was hired, but now I felt my newfound legitimacy would be on the line if I couldn't give the right answer on the spot.

I learned a valuable lesson as I tried to be the go-to source for sports news. One day, in the throes of my research, Krummie popped into my office with a question about a college defensive player who would be entering the draft that year. I was watching a video and didn't hear his question completely, but I could tell that the inquiry required a yes or no answer.

"Yep," I responded, barely looking up from my computer screen.

Two days later, Krummie sat in the seat across from my desk. He wasn't smiling.

"Let me give you a piece of advice, rook. If you don't know the answer to something, then say, 'I don't know,' you got me?"

"Yes, sir," I said as I struggled to make eye contact.

He stood up and walked out, obviously not pleased to have found that my answer had been incorrect.

That episode stressed the importance of not only having an answer, but of having the *right* answer. Sometimes the right answer is, "I don't know, but I will get that information for you ASAP." Granted, it is difficult for most people to admit they don't know. You may even feel like your job security or advancement hinges on your ability to answer questions posed by your superiors. While I understand the stress this can create, the right approach is to always be as honest about what you don't know as you are about what you do know. My five years in Cambridge, Massachusetts, exposed me to legions of people who had to have the answer to any question at any time. While most people place a premium on having an answer, I realized very quickly that it was better to be trusted. The urge and desire to have an answer for every question can be overwhelming, but it must be tamed.

# THE MYTHICAL OFFSEASON

In March of 2008, I was working as hard as I had worked in October of 2007. NFL games wouldn't resume for another seven months, but that didn't matter. There was a pile of work on the corner of my desk and it was steadily rising to the ceiling. Many of my friends assumed that I had the schedule of a high school teacher with three months of summer vacation. Not so in the NFL. The calendar had just enough milestones during the "offseason" to occupy large swaths of time. The Combine took place in February.[28] The NFL Draft happened in April. Shortly thereafter, we would bring rookies in for a minicamp. Then we would bring the entire team together for another camp. We got a few weeks in July for "vacation" before reporting for training camp in the last week of the month.

This schedule was not for the faint of heart. It was general knowledge that one never called in sick. If you were sick, you made a visit to the team physician, took a few meds, and got right back to your office. In a machismo-dominated world where we were demanding players be tough, we couldn't show any chinks in our own armor.

As the NFL Combine neared, the anticipation for the organization continued to build. This Combine would be a pivotal moment in the trajectory of the team. The subsequent draft would give us an opportunity to get back into the playoff hunt. Herm made one thing very clear to the coaching staff in our first offseason meeting: "These kids we bring in for the draft are going to play. We are not going to put them on the bench. I want us to select players who will be able to play quickly for us. At 4–12, we don't have the luxury of storing

28    The NFL Combine is an annual showcase of college football players who are entering the NFL Draft.

players on the shelf. Let's get some guys in here who can contribute early. When you watch college tape and interview these guys in Indy, figure out if he can contribute *now*. Not later. *Now*."

There were rumors that our front office was on a hunt to accumulate as many picks in the draft as possible. The draft selection process included seven rounds, with each team in the League slated to get one pick in each round. For a club to accumulate more picks, it had to get them from other teams, usually through trades or as a "compensatory pick" from the league. With a 4–12 record, everyone was potential trade material. No one was untouchable. It would be an interesting spring.

## THE DRAFT

On April 22, 2008, an intern walked into my office and said, "We traded Jared Allen to the Vikings."

I was watching film in my dimly lit office, a hoodie pulled over my head. I was somewhere in the netherworld between slight consciousness and slumber. Upon hearing his news, I sat upright and threw my hood back.

"What?"

"We traded Jared Allen."

Although I understood the words that were coming out of his mouth, I didn't want to believe what he was saying. Allen was our star. He was a mullet-sporting defensive end whom we had drafted from Idaho State in 2004 as a fourth-rounder. It didn't take long to realize we had picked a true gem. In our 2007 season, a year that featured very few highlights, Allen sparkled. He led the NFL in sacks

(15.5) and was selected to represent the AFC as the starting defensive end. Oh, and he caught two touchdown passes on offense. He was a rare talent—a combination of size (six foot six and 255 pounds) and athleticism. Now he was headed to the Minnesota Vikings in exchange for one first-round pick, two third-round picks, and a swap of sixth-round picks. The Vikings promptly signed him to the richest defensive contract at the time—a $72.6 million, six-year deal.

We were four days from the draft.

The Allen trade raised our draft number to twelve picks, tying us with the Bears for the most number of picks. All eyes would be on us. The tension crept upward. As we put the finishing touches on our draft board, scouts battled with coaches and coaches battled with scouts over our internal ranking of players.

Every team had a board that listed every player entering the draft and ranked them by their desirability and relative value to other teams. Three draft approaches dominated strategy development for NFL teams. First, a team could decide to fill only team needs with their picks. This process involved evaluating the gap areas on a squad and then seeking to fill those gaps with players in the draft. The second approach was to "take the best player on the board." The justification for this philosophy is that a team should always take the best players available at the time. The third was a combination of the first two approaches. Essentially, a team matched needs with talent available and made its picks accordingly.

This thought process has resonance in other areas of life, especially for organizations and individuals who need to find skilled talent. There is always a desire to fill a gap immediately with the best talent that is available. But perhaps the cost of waiting until better talent emerges in the marketplace is less than the cost of filling the gap quickly. The important takeaway is to create a comprehensive map of the talent pool available at any given time. Even if the current state of affairs seems good, it is important to be ready to strike with precision when the need to fill a position arises.

Behind closed doors, we simulated draft-day scenarios. Our first pick was at the number five spot, so four teams—Miami, St. Louis, Atlanta, and Oakland—would select players before us. Once Miami drafted the first player, the rest of the teams would begin to reorganize the board. With the vitality of a War College simulation, the scouts, general manager, and head coach ran an endless list of simulations. What if the Raiders picked Chris Long, a defensive end from the University of Virginia? Or what if the Rams took Sedrick Ellis, a defensive tackle from the University of Southern California? All of these decisions would trigger various shuffles and result in drastically different answers. As a peon, I was not privy to which players were most valued by our draft brain trust. All I knew was that we had twelve opportunities to get the team back in the winner's column.

This felt like a make-or-break moment, and anyone who has been in the throes of a company trying to fight its way to survival knows the feeling. While there's an excitement in rolling the dice, there's always a little fear that the wrong numbers could get you kicked out of the casino.

The two-day draft garnered a dozen new Chiefs from across the country. LSU, Clemson, and Virginia were just a few of the big-name colleges we drew from. We also pulled from small programs (Brandon Carr from Grand Valley State). Within a week of the draft, everyone was accounted for. Now it was time to go to work.

. . .

We had the not-so-good fortune of playing the New England Patriots on the road in our first game of the 2008 season. It was their first game after losing the Super Bowl to the New York Giants. They had finished the 2007 season 18–1. This would also be my first big challenge—creating a scouting report on the Patriots based on their last four games of the 2007 season. This involved watching nearly 300 football plays. I had to both label and draw each play.

I was stressed. This was going to be my first major test for Professor Gun. I felt like a doctoral student preparing to defend his dissertation. I pulled all-nighter after all-nighter, downing Red Bulls with the need of a crack addict.

Finally, I peeked into his office. "Gun, I'm done."

"You sure?"

"Yes, I'm done. Everything is in the computer."

"Okay, let's take a look at it. Get all of the coaches together for a defensive staff meeting at one, after lunch."

My heart dropped. The whole defensive staff was going to review my work. I started to sweat.

"We're gonna meet at one in the staff room to watch the Patriots tape" was my standard line as I trudged from office to office.

When I got to Gibby's office, he had a big smile on his face.

"I already know. You ready for what's about to happen?" he asked. "Everybody has to go through this at least once. It won't be fun, and you will learn a lot. Take notes."

I couldn't muster the breath to say "thank you." I just kept walking.

When the meeting started, Gun turned off the lights and pulled up my reel of plays. Each play showed two views. There was a setting that allowed the viewer to see the label of the player (how I had identified it) in bright yellow text at the bottom of the screen. Of course, Gun chose to show it.

He nestled into his chair and pressed Play. Ten seconds into the inquisition, he hit the Pause button.

"This is wrong," he said. "You called it Doubles Left 36 Lead. It's Doubles Right 37 Wham."

From the tone of his voice, I knew this was going to be a long meeting.

For the next three hours, Gun demolished all of my work from the previous three weeks. Although the other coaches in the room heard his voice, to my ear it sounded as if a wrecking ball was making contact with the side of a skyscraper every time he opened his mouth. By my calculation, I had spent close to 250 hours on this project. I braced for more.

I sucked it up and just kept writing. I kept shoving my pride under the table. My clothes were drenched from sweat and my psyche was riddled with bullet holes, but I kept writing.

At the end of the session, the rest of the coaches exited the room. I was left with Gun.

"D, you've been in the League for fifteen seconds. I know some veteran coaches who would have made some of the mistakes that you made. Get over it and make the corrections," Gun said.

That episode underscored the value of a good mentor. A mentor will speak the truth even when it may bring you to tears. He or she only asks in return that you try to stay humble and coachable.

I went back to my office and spent the next nine hours correcting each and every play based on the notes I had taken. I finished up at midnight. As soon as the final play was done, I reprinted the reports and walked into each coach's office. I picked up the old report and replaced it with the new report.

The next morning, Gibby peeked his head in my office.

"Smart man, you fixed that crap quick. I like it."

After a solid week of practice, we made our way to Gillette Stadium. "The House that Brady Built" was loudly anticipating its hero's emergence from the tunnel. As I stood on the sideline, putting a few of our defensive backs through a pregame workout, the unmistakable introduction to Jay Z's "Public Service Announcement" played on the PA. On cue, Tom Brady and his entourage of backup quarterbacks ran onto the field for warm-ups. The pregame crowd went wild.

We lost to Brady and the Patriots that day by a score of 17–10. Without going into panic mode, we regrouped and readied for Oakland's arrival in the second week. Although no one would say it, the impossible seemed impossible. There was no way we could lose to the Raiders again. But we did. That game spelled the beginning of the end for us. As the losses mounted, we began to break the wrong kinds of records. We became the first Chiefs team to begin three consecutive seasons 0–2. We ran the longest losing streak in franchise history—twelve games. Our quarterback, Brodie Croyle, suffered a season-ending injury in week seven, and from there our season spiraled out of control.

2–14. That was the final tally for a season in which we had the highest hopes with the youngest roster in the NFL. Our average starting age was 25.5. It was a certainty that the firings I witnessed the first year would be multiplied. Our general manager announced his resignation, effective at season's end. The writing was on the wall for our coaching staff. The general consensus in professional sports is that if there is a change of general manager, the coaching staff will be the next to get shown the door.

As soon as the season ended, coaches began going into bunker mode. Office doors that had stayed open during the entire season were now closed. Muffled conversations could be overheard in the hallway as coaches began to reach out to their agents and other coaching buddies. The writing was on the wall. We were about to get a new general manager, and after that, it would only be a matter of time.

Gun walked into my office, closed the door, and sat across from my desk.

"Listen, Daron, you're going to be fine. Don't take a job anywhere else. You can interview, just don't take a job anywhere else. Trust me."

He stood up and walked away.

As soon as he left, I turned to my computer screen and sent an email to my mentor and good friend, Kent. I trusted Gun, but I trusted myself even more. I had been coaching in the League long enough to know that when the music stops, there will be some coaches left standing without a chair to grab. I wouldn't let myself be that guy.

"It looks like only a matter of time before the coaches get axed," I wrote. "Can you reach out to McCarthy for me?"

Kent's response: "Of course. Hold tight."

The next day, news started to surface that Scott Pioli, vice president of player personnel for the New England Patriots, would be our new GM. Knowing Pioli as a disciple of Bill Belichick, we all knew that our days in the sun were over. Pioli's philosophy was antithetical to Herm's approach. The bomb was about to get detonated.

Ten days after Pioli was hired, Herm was fired. Assistant coaches started to jump overboard. Gibby finagled some way out of his contract and went to the Texans as defensive backs coach. Paralyzed by the fear among the remaining staffers in the building, I refused to leave my desk. I'd go to the office armed with three meals—breakfast, lunch, and dinner—so I wouldn't have to leave my desk, save for an emergency bathroom break. I was hoping that I could fly under the radar as the lowest-level coaching assistant and just join the incoming staff. That plan sounded good, but I knew it was next to impossible.

And then I caught my lifeline.

Kent's email read: "Here is the email address for McCarthy's secretary. He wants you to visit Green Bay."

I almost jumped out of my chair. This was exactly what I needed.

## THE PACK

Within forty-eight hours, I was sitting in Mike McCarthy's office. His arms were resting on the same desk that Vince Lombardi had once used. He grilled me on everything I had done for the Chiefs since my first day on the team. Had I worked with special teams? Answer: Yes. Did I know how to draw offensive, defensive, and special teams plays using PlayMaker? Answer: Yes. Had I put together scouting reports? Answer: Yes. Would I feel comfortable working with the offense? Answer: Yes.

My approach to this interview was simply to say yes to any question that pertained to my ability or desire to perform a function for the Green Bay Packers. If McCarthy had asked me if I had ever done any scaffolding work for the Chiefs, I would say yes. Some may describe my approach as disingenuous. I can understand that. All I knew at the time was that I wasn't going to leave that building until I had a job offer. Period.

There's one lesson here: Do whatever you have to do (short of picking up a felony) to get into the building. My theory on life is that no one actually knows what he or she is doing; some are better at faking it than others.

When I got back to the hotel after the day-long interview, I got a call from Mike. He had a position for me. It was exactly the same pay and position as the job I was leaving in Kansas City. I took it. We would work out contract details. I was going to be a Green Bay Packer.

The next morning, as I headed for the airport, I got a call from an unidentified number. I don't usually answer calls from unknown numbers, but I went against my practice and answered it anyway.

"Daron, where are you?" Gun asked.

"In Green Bay, headed to the airport."

"You didn't take a job, did you?" he asked.

"Well, yeah, I did. Mike offered me a job and I took it. Nothing has been shaking loose for me, so I took the first thing I could get."

"Well, now you have to call Mike and turn the position down."

"What?" I blurted out. The cab driver was beginning to frown at me in the rearview mirror.

"I just took the defensive coordinator's job with Detroit. You're the only coach I'm bringing with me. You will be the assistant defensive backs coach. You need to be on a plane to Detroit on Monday."

"What the hell?" I felt lightheaded. I was excited, pissed off, and scared at the same time. I was already grimacing over the conversation I was going to have with Coach McCarthy, but I had to turn him down.

"Okay, Gun, I'm in."

"Of course you're in! Our secretary will call you to set up a flight, moving trucks, and all that other stuff. We're going to turn this thing around. See you in Michigan."

He hung up.

Before I could talk myself out of the hard work that I needed to do, I called McCarthy. It was short and sweet. I needed to go to Detroit. It was a better offer and would give me a chance to actually coach NFL players.

"Well, good luck," he said and hung up.

Next, I called Kent and narrated the entire chain of events. I wanted to make sure he understood my thought process.

His response was what I hoped it would be: "D, you gotta make the best decision for you. I'm happy for you."

And with that, I was headed to the Detroit Lions—a team that had finished 0–16 the previous season. They were the worst team in the League, but it was the best job offer I got. In just over a year and a half, I had gone from a guy who had never played a snap of professional or college football to an assistant position coach in the NFL. Location was a minor detail. I was headed to Motown.

## PIVOT POINTS

1   Know your status. When you're not in a position to negotiate, *don't negotiate.*

2   Sometimes the best answer is, "I don't know, but I will get that information for you ASAP."

3   Don't be afraid to ask people to hit the Pause button. If the information is important, then make sure you get it.

4   You are expendable. Have an exit strategy even when you're having the best season of your life.

5   Push your pride under the table. Fix mistakes quickly.

6   Give yourself a chance to be disappointed. Keep taking gambles. You only have to be right once (Mark Cuban).

# AFTERWORD

My son sauntered into the kitchen at 6 a.m. as only a three-year-old could—clumsily. It was February of 2014 and I was fresh from getting fired by the Cleveland Browns.

"Hello, Dylan," I said. I couldn't see him, and he didn't respond, but I could sense him getting closer. Soon, he was standing right beside me.

"You eat breakfast?" he asked.

"What?" I shot back in an annoyed tone.

"You," he said while punching the air with his pointer finger. "Youuuu eeeaat breakfast?" To ensure that I understood what he was saying, he pointed back and forth from me to the pan of scrambled eggs.

That's when I got it. He had never seen me eat breakfast. Actually, I'm sure he had, but it had occurred so infrequently that his mind had not recorded it as a normal event.

I dropped my spatula, sat down on the floor, and cried.

In the course of those two minutes, I realized that I had spent the majority of the previous seven years coaching the sons of *other* people. My 4 a.m. departures and midnight returns had prevented me from spending quality time with the most important son in my life—Dylan.

I loved coaching, but I couldn't reconcile not having the time to *coach* my own son. So I decided to take a year off and teach a course at UT. Making that decision was more difficult than getting into coaching, but I needed to regroup. I called my own audible.

Within four weeks of submitting a syllabus to the University of Texas, we packed and headed south to Austin. We found a great month-to-month lease and unpacked for a new life in the city. In the fall I would begin my appointment as a lecturer in the Liberal Arts Honors Program, teaching a sports leadership seminar.

■ ■ ■

And then, just as the fall semester was getting under way, TMZ released the surveillance video of the infamous Ray Rice episode. The footage showed Rice, a Baltimore Ravens running back, leveling his girlfriend, Janay Palmer, with a punch to the face. The incident ignited a national conversation about domestic violence.

Within weeks, Roger Goodell, the NFL commissioner, visited UT's football coach, Charlie Strong. Given Strong's hard-line stance and reputation as a disciplinarian, the visit made sense. My invitation was a surprise, even though I had known Commissioner Goodell since my time in Detroit.

The conversation between two of the most powerful men in sports orbited the very issue I was preaching in my classroom: the need for leadership and character development for athletes and coaches. That conversation sparked an idea in me: Why not create an institute that would leverage UT's academic *and* sports capital?

We could create a leadership model for college athletes and deploy that system to high school players.

I had already written the blueprint while coaching for the Detroit Lions. I created a nonprofit football camp, 4th and 1, that combined football coaching with ACT prep and life skills development for high schoolers.[29] Between camps in Michigan, Florida, and Texas, we had reached more than 500 young men. A typical day involved a two-mile run, a yoga class, football practice, a three-hour ACT prep, a session on meal etiquette, and a social media branding workshop. Why not bring that model to the next level at UT?

■ ■ ■

I took the idea to UT's president, Bill Powers, in October 2014. A scheduled thirty-minute discussion turned into an hour, and then another hour. On December 15, we stood shoulder-to-shoulder to announce the creation of the Center for Sports Leadership & Innovation (CSLI).

As the founding director, I created a three-hour course for UT's freshmen athletes. The syllabus revolved around leadership and financial literacy and the readings ranged from Machiavelli's *The Prince* to Brené Brown's *Daring Greatly*. In just under twelve months, we trained more than four hundred athletes and coaches in areas ranging from leadership to financial management. Now in our second year, we are on track to spread the movement around the entire country.

But, most important, every Saturday that I am home (which is most of the year), I attend the Donut Council with my three oldest

29    www.4thand1.org

kids. Every Friday night, we scout out donut shops on Google, select an unlucky target, and descend upon the establishment when the doors open the next morning. Dressed in our bright red T-shirts, we order mounds of donuts, talk about current events, and have a great time.[30] The Donut Council is the highlight of my week, and an extension of my leadership philosophy: Lead by example and mentor through engagement.

I am spending life with the people I care about most. And that has made all the difference.

30    Visit us at www.donutcouncil.org.

# ABOUT THE AUTHOR

Daron K. Roberts is a fifth-generation East Texan and the son of a Baptist minister and an elementary school principal. When Daron was seven, his father took out a map of Panola County drawn in the late 1800s. Panola County sent one company of soldiers to fight for the Confederacy during the Civil War. The map showed that Bill Roberts, Daron's great-great-grandfather, owned approximately 150 acres in 1870, just five years removed from the end of the war. Daron's father rolled up the map and simply said, "This is why you will never have any excuses."

Daron's path from East Texas followed the trajectory of his dad's proclamation. He was elected class president all four years in high school and served as student body president at the University of Texas in 2000—the largest student body in the nation at the time. After graduating from the Plan II Honors program, Daron ventured to the nation's capital to work as an aide to Senator Joe Lieberman. He earned a master in public policy degree from the Harvard Kennedy School of Government in 2004—the same year he was finally accepted into Harvard Law School after being wait-listed for three years.

During the summer before his last year in law school, Roberts decided to double down on his newfound desire to become a football coach. When the Kansas City Chiefs took him up on his offer to work for free, Roberts began making his dream a reality. Seven years and multiple NFL teams later, Roberts returned to the University of Texas to teach sports leadership courses and created the Center for Sports Leadership and Innovation. Through the Center, Roberts crafted a cutting-edge curriculum—Gameplan for Winning at Life—that combines the leading research on connection, resilience, influence, and financial literacy. He teaches the course to all freshman athletes at the University of Texas. In addition to making nearly fifty speeches to audiences across the globe each year, Roberts is also the host of *A Tribe Called Yes*, a podcast that unearths the narratives of the world's most famous risk-takers.

Daron and his incredibly beautiful and patient wife, Hilary, have four children: Dylan, Sydney, Jackson, and Delaney. They are undecided on whether or not they will uphold a premarriage commitment to have five kids.

Roberts has touched all seven continents, and yes, that includes Antarctica.

# BOOK DARON K. ROBERTS
# AS YOUR KEYNOTE SPEAKER

*"Daron's talk was riveting, heartfelt, and jam-packed with actionable content for members of our team."*

**—SENIOR EXECUTIVE PARTICIPANT,**
CORNELL UNIVERSITY

As a keynote speaker, Daron consistently provides an energetic message that simultaneously entertains his audience and inspires them to create lasting positive change.

**Appeals to a Wide Range of Audiences.** Daron has wowed audiences from executive gatherings to athletic departments, association conferences, and leadership seminars.

**Delivers Powerful Tools.** Daron is *not a motivational speaker*. He delivers inspirational content that will provoke your audience to successfully navigate their next transition.

**Tailors the Message.** Daron adapts the versatile power of his story to the specific needs of your audience.

To bring Daron K. Roberts to your organization

VISIT WWW.DARONKROBERTS.COM